T0013184

Raising Kids to Follow Christ by Lee Ann Mancini is a much-needed resource for the times in which we find ourselves. As Mancini so accurately states, "Christianity is being attacked on every imaginable level..." Indeed. More than ever, parents—and every adult believer with influence in the lives of children—must be committed to imparting a thoroughly biblical view of life and faith. Lee Ann Mancini is a compelling voice that God has raised up to inspire and equip. It is a joy to recommend her book, and I pray that countless numbers of people will benefit from her work.

—Alex McFarland
Author, educator, religion correspondent

Raising Kids to Follow Christ is a must-read for parents wanting to build a strong spiritual foundation in their children. Lee Ann Mancini's expertly crafted guide offers practical strategies and biblical insights, making it an invaluable resource to nurture faith within the family.

—Ryan Frank
CEO and publisher, KidzMatter

Lee Ann Mancini has penned a well-researched, extensive handbook for parenting with a biblically based worldview. Lee Ann has captured the heart of the Creator toward parents and children. Wisdom, compassion, love, truth, and beauty are woven throughout this power-packed parenting manual. If you are a parent who wants *more* for your children, grandchildren, and the next generation, this guide will equip you to train and transform them to grow leaders and lovers of Christ and the church and bring hope to a world that needs revival, redemption, and restoration by providing authentic Christians as bright lights reflecting the Savior and His heart for humankind.

—Pam Farrel
Codirector, Love-Wise
Coauthor, *The 10 Best Decisions Every Parent Can Make*

This remarkable book holds the keys to establishing a spiritual bedrock in your child's life. It blends practical wisdom with biblical principles and provides a comprehensive roadmap, empowering you to foster a lifelong connection to faith within your child. It's a great read for every Christian parent.

—*Dr. Scott Turansky*
Cofounder, National Center for Biblical Parenting

Many Christian parents want to pass along their faith to their children yet feel ill-equipped to do that. Author Lee Ann Mancini shows parents how to set the stage to influence and encourage their children's faith development. *Raising Kids to Follow Christ* is filled with biblical strategies and techniques crafted to awaken and grow that faith. This book is the tool you want to be the spiritual leader your child needs.

—*Lori Wildenberg*
Parent coach
Author, *The Messy Life of Parenting*

What could be more important in parenting than raising children who know Christ? Our kids must decide their eternal destiny for themselves, but we can certainly create a home environment where it's hard to deny the truth and love of God. The world says academic excellence, good looks, or athletic prowess will set up our kids for success. This book reminds us of what is truly important in life: to obey the Lord and follow Him.

—*Arlene Pellicane*
Author, *Parents Rising*
Host, *Happy Home Podcast*

What a wonderful gift Lee Ann Mancini has provided in *Raising Kids to Follow Christ*. Lee Ann has the heart of a shepherd and the wisdom of a seasoned parent. She provides practical guidance to parents with children at every age and stage. If you've got parenting figured out, then this book is not for you. For the rest of us, here is good medicine that will help us raise children who know, love, and serve Jesus for a lifetime.

—*Dr. Josh Mulvihill*
Executive director, Renewanation
Author, *Biblical Grandparenting*

Raising children in today's world is hard—much harder than I expected it to be when I became a mom eighteen-plus years ago. Though sin has been prevalent since the fall of man, the ideologies our kids are exposed to and the societal pressures placed on them from today's media are unprecedented. More than ever, parents must be intentional about finding every opportunity to point their children to their Savior, and it doesn't happen by chance. We cannot count on the church or schools to do it. It's our responsibility, and it is a calling that, if not taken seriously, can have eternal consequences. *Raising Kids to Follow Christ* is full of biblical wisdom and practical advice. Lee Ann shares from her own personal experiences as a mom who raised her own kids to follow Christ, but more importantly, she guides parents through what Scripture says about parenting and discipleship. This book is certain to reach the hearts of both new and experienced parents and will no doubt be a resource I will return to time and time again.

—*Yvette Hampton*
Producer and host, *Schoolhouse Rocked: The Homeschool Revolution*

In a world of compromise and confusion, *Raising Kids to Follow Christ* is the timely resource you need. Author Lee Ann Mancini says, "One of the most important decisions parents will make is how to raise their children to become strong, Bible-based disciples of Jesus." Raising kids to follow Christ doesn't just happen—it requires wisdom, resolve, and a biblical foundation. This book offers practical parenting principles and engaging stories to help you partner with Christ to raise strong Christian kids.

—*Rhonda Stoppe*
Podcast host, *Old Ladies Know Stuff*
Author, *Moms Raising Sons to Be Men*

RAISING KIDS TO FOLLOW CHRIST

Instilling a Lifelong Trust in God

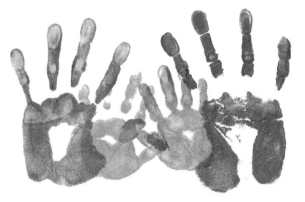

LEE ANN MANCINI

WHITAKER
HOUSE

Unless otherwise indicated, all Scripture quotations are taken from the *Holy Bible, New International Version*®, NIV®, © 1973, 1978, 1984, 2011 by Biblica, Inc.® Used by permission of Zondervan. All rights reserved worldwide. www.zondervan.com. The "NIV" and "New International Version" are trademarks registered in the United States Patent and Trademark Office by Biblica, Inc.® Scripture quotations marked (ESV) are taken from *The Holy Bible, English Standard Version*, © 2016, 2001, 2000, 1995 by Crossway Bibles, a division of Good News Publishers. Used by permission. All rights reserved. Scripture quotations marked (NKJV) are taken from the *New King James Version*, © 1982 by Thomas Nelson, Inc. Used by permission. All rights reserved. Scripture quotations marked (NLT) are taken from the *Holy Bible, New Living Translation*, © 1996, 2004, 2015 by Tyndale House Foundation. Used by permission of Tyndale House Publishers, Inc., Carol Stream, Illinois 60188. All rights reserved.

Boldface type in the Scripture quotations indicates the author's emphasis.

RAISING KIDS TO FOLLOW CHRIST
Instilling a Lifelong Trust in God

raisingchristiankids.com
leeannmancini.com

ISBN: 979-8-88769-094-0
eBook ISBN: 979-8-88769-095-7
Printed in the United States of America
© 2024 by Lee Ann Mancini

Whitaker House
1030 Hunt Valley Circle
New Kensington, PA 15068
www.whitakerhouse.com

Library of Congress Cataloging-in-Publication Data
Names: Mancini, Lee Ann, 1958– author.
Title: Raising kids to follow Christ : instilling a lifelong trust in God /
    Lee Ann Mancini.
Description: New Kensington, PA : Whitaker House, [2024] | Summary: "Using
    real-life examples and stories from the Bible, author provides
    suggestions for teaching moments, strategies, techniques, and
    disciplinary practices to change children's hearts so that they become
    effective disciples for Christ"— Provided by publisher.
Identifiers: LCCN 2023041532 (print) | LCCN 2023041533 (ebook) | ISBN
    9798887690940 | ISBN 9798887690957 (ebook)
Subjects: LCSH: Child rearing—Religious aspects—Christianity. |
    Parenting—Religious aspects—Christianity. | BISAC: RELIGION /
    Christian Living / Parenting | RELIGION / Christian Ministry /
    Discipleship
Classification: LCC BV4529 .M345 2024 (print) | LCC BV4529 (ebook) | DDC
    248.8/45—dc23/eng/20231109
LC record available at https://lccn.loc.gov/2023041532
LC ebook record available at https://lccn.loc.gov/2023041533

No part of this book may be reproduced or transmitted in any form or by any means, electronic or mechanical—including photocopying, recording, or by any information storage and retrieval system—without permission in writing from the publisher. Please direct your inquiries to permissionseditor@whitakerhouse.com.

2 3 4 5 6 7 8 9 10 11 12 **ᴜ** 31 30 29 28 27 26 25 24

DEDICATION

To Guy and Lena, I am eternally grateful and blessed God chose me to be your mother. I love you beyond comprehension.

To all who dedicate their lives to shaping their children's hearts and minds to love the Lord. May God continue to bless you.

To Kirsten and Crystal for their unwavering support, guidance, and dedication. Thank you for your help in making this book a reality.

And to the Lord for His many blessings as He continues to direct my steps personally and professionally so I will one day hear, "Well done, faithful servant."

CONTENTS

FOREWORD

I attended church with my family throughout my childhood. I enjoyed Sunday school and church camp. I was confirmed along with cousins and friends. But I didn't know Jesus.

I listened to lessons and sermons loosely based on the Bible but didn't know I could read the Bible too. I heard stories about God but didn't know I should be learning Truth. I didn't learn anything about the Holy Spirit. Most lessons about Jesus occurred twice a year, on Easter and Christmas.

I sang songs with others but didn't know I was supposed to worship God. I listened to pastors pray scripted prayers but didn't understand I could pray too.

When I was young, no one taught me I could have a personal relationship with Jesus Christ, God's Son, through faith in God the Father, and that His Holy Spirit would indwell me to empower me. My parents didn't know either. They did the best they could. I'm grateful they raised my brother and me in church and eventually came to faith and trusted Christ. My brother and I trusted Christ as young adults so we're enjoying living out the abundant life here on earth Jesus sacrificed for us to have.

I've often wondered how different and more beautiful our lives would be if our parents had loved God, known Jesus, and raised my brother and me to do the same. I no longer wonder after talking with Lee Ann and reading this significant book. I understand how much better off I would have been. Assurance. Confidence. Security. Passion. Joy. Love. Wisdom. Guidance. Support. Relationship. Peace. Connected family.

From our first conversation about this book, I knew it needed to be written, and Lee Ann needed to write it. There's nothing like this, and no one quite like Lee Ann.

She loves God profoundly and desperately wants every child to know Him, believe in Him, and love Him. This passion motivated her to do the necessary research that sets this book apart. She will convince you that young children are more capable of understanding and believing than you realize. She wrote, edited, and rewrote so you would have the book you're holding.

Lee Ann's respect for parents comes through on these pages. She believes in you and wants you to experience the joy of discipling your children so they know and trust Christ as soon as possible and grow in wisdom, love, character, and obedience. Lee Ann will explain what you need to believe. She'll inspire you to try her ideas. She'll prepare you to make changes so you can successfully apply her instruction. Get ready for relevant Scriptures, essential statistics, vibrant illustrations, scripted prayers, life-giving cautions, explicit instruction, meaningful quotes, age-appropriate definitions, descriptions to share with your children, and more.

I pray you take Lee Ann's instruction as seriously as she did the writing of this masterpiece. Your children are worth it! We want them to know the goodness of God from the very beginning. It will change them!

—*Dr. Kathy Koch*
Founder, Celebrate Kids, Inc.
Author, *Parent Differently* and *Resilient Kids*

INTRODUCTION

I feel certain that most parents vividly remember holding their babies for the first time. I know I do! Before my son Guy was born, I promised God that I would raise him to know and love God the Father, Son, and Holy Spirit. As they placed my son on my chest, my first words were, "Thank You, Jesus!" Then I said, "Wow, look at his big hands!" I envisioned him folding his hands together and praying to the Lord as a lifelong follower of Christ.

The most valuable gifts from our Lord are the beautiful children He has given us, created in His image. The most valuable gift we can give to our Lord is to be equipped, empowered, and filled with the Holy Spirit to help raise His children to be lifelong followers of Christ. Joel 1:3 states, *"Tell it to your children, and let your children tell it to their children, and their children to the next generation."* There is nothing more important than raising our children to love and obey the Lord all of their lives so that they, in turn, will raise their children to do the same. This is how we make disciples. (See Matthew 28:19–20.)

Just for a moment, imagine being in heaven, sitting at God's divine banquet table, looking around for your child...who's nowhere to be found. Jonathan Edwards, a North American revivalist preacher in the 1700s, deliberately tried to frighten parents with this same thought.[1] When I first read that, it shook me to my core because it never crossed my mind that my children might not be in heaven with me for all eternity. This disturbing thought should help us realize the importance of doing all that we can, to the best of our abilities, to connect our children's hearts to Christ. I prayed that I would raise my children in a godly home, according to God's directives in His Word, and that they would believe in the Lord by honoring and serving Him all the days of their lives. It's the most important and blessed duty the Lord has assigned to us.

In his book, *Raising Spiritual Champions*,[2] George Barna shares some startling statistics. Barna says that among children thirteen to fourteen years old:

+ 70 percent either reject the existence of Satan or don't know if he exists.

+ 90 percent believe there are no absolute moral truths.

+ 83 percent do not believe we are born into sin and need salvation.

+ Less than 1 percent of early teens have a biblical worldview. The prevailing worldview among 99 percent of young teens is syncretism, a combination of different beliefs.

As for their parents:

+ 68 percent think of themselves as Christian, but only 2 percent have a true biblical worldview.

---

1. Catherine A. Brekus, "Children of Wrath, Children of Grace: Jonathan Edwards and the Puritan Culture of Child Rearing," in *The Child in Christian Thought*, ed. Marcia J. Bunge (Grand Rapids, MI: Wm. B. Eerdmans Publishing Co. 2001), 322.
2. George Barna, *Raising Spiritual Champions: Nurturing Your Child's Heart, Mind and Soul* (Glendale, AZ: Arizona Christian University Press & Fedd Books, 2023).

+ Less than half of all born-again adults (45 percent) read or study the Bible weekly.

+ Only 25 percent of parents believe absolute moral truths exist.

According to Barna, the statistics are not much better when it comes to children's pastors:

+ 64 percent believe there is no absolute moral truth.

+ 53 percent accept reincarnation as a real possibility for them.

+ 50 percent believe that Jesus sinned while He was on earth.

+ 43 percent do not believe that people are born into sin and need Jesus Christ to overcome the effects of sin.

Barna warns, "Today we are at the precipice of irreversible self-destruction."[3] Aristotle reportedly said, "Give me a child until the age of seven, and they will be mine the rest of their lives." Hitler, Mussolini, Lenin, and Stalin believed this as well.[4]

But there is good news. Along with your prayers and the Word of God, I pray the book you are holding in your hands can help change the trajectory of how we raise the next generation.

For everyone raising children, the years of childhood pass by quickly. As a parent, grandparent, extended family member, ministry leader, or teacher, we are called to teach, guide, and instruct the next generation. We are our children's first and most impactful teachers, the principal educators who can help anchor their lives in Jesus now and for eternity.

It is my prayer that the information in this book will help prepare you to be the very best spiritual leader for your child. I have

---

3. Ibid., 44.
4. Ibid., 52.

included transformational, educational, and, most importantly, biblical directives to empower and equip you.

This is the truth that all of us must live by if we hope that our children will follow in our footsteps. By living according to the Word of God, we can set a good example for children and help them grow up to become God-loving and God-fearing adults. Only by understanding and applying the Word of God can we truly teach them God's Word—the foundation upon which all knowledge and behavior are built.

Jesus is the living cornerstone, *"the living Stone...chosen by God and precious to him"* (1 Peter 2:4); He holds your child's soul safe and secure. So when the storms of life bring devastating consequences or false doctrine, trying to entice your children away from God, they will stand strong in faith, hope, and love. They will be anchored body, mind, and soul in the Lord Jesus Christ.

Although I address parents throughout the book, it is written for anyone doing the most important job on earth: raising, nurturing, and supporting the next generation to become lifelong believers and disciples. Because we can know the Father only through the Son, I have emphasized the importance of building a strong relationship with Jesus. Whatever I say about God also applies to Jesus and the Holy Spirit because they are one holy Trinity.

Also, each child is unique and learns differently, so methods that work for one child may not work for another. Children have distinct cognitive abilities; some children grasp concepts quickly while others do so at a slower pace. Children may be active learners, passive learners, or a combination of both. Their environment can also impact their learning capacity and retention rate because some children thrive in a noisy environment while others excel in a quiet atmosphere.

As you read about building a strong foundation in Christ before the age of seven—which is a completion number in the economy of God—you will also understand that it is never too early nor too late to help your children learn to love Jesus and accept Him as their Savior. Many of the ideas that I share can be tweaked to apply to all ages. You may have to change the suggested guidelines to accommodate a child with special psychological or physical needs.

The goal of this book is to give you a thorough understanding of God's directives and share ideas that have stood the test of time, as well as provide fresh and informative ideas that will help you raise your child to become a lifelong believer in Christ and help transform the world. I want to inspire caretakers to unleash their God-given potential and increase their biblical wisdom—influenced by the Holy Spirit—to guide and lead future generations.

God has promised to *"equip you with everything good for doing his will"* (Hebrews 13:21), and He will just as assuredly equip you to raise the next generation to believe in Him, His Son, and His Holy Spirit.

We must be vigilant in raising our children to be prepared to stand strong in faith against the anti-Christian culture. We must instill in them a love for God and His Word and a desire to live according to His principles. Above all, we must pray for our children to remain strong in their faith and one day be able to impact the world for Christ. *"Through the praise of children and infants you have established a stronghold against your enemies"* (Psalm 8:2).

1

THE PERFECT CORNERSTONE
AND FOUNDATION

The Sand Palace is a beautiful home built on the shore in Mexico Beach, Florida. On October 10, 2018, Hurricane Michael, a category 5 hurricane with winds reaching 160 mph, tore through and destroyed the Florida Panhandle. Mexico Beach was one of the hardest-hit areas, where homes and businesses were decimated, leaving nothing but bare foundations. However, the Sand Palace was largely untouched, standing tall on its stilts above the carnage and destruction all around. Everyone wanted to know why this home survived in such pristine condition.

The homeowners of the Sand Palace were wise enough to build their home to withstand 240 to 250 mph winds, despite Florida's state code that requires houses to be built to withstand 120 mph winds. Instead of 30-foot pilings, the Sand Palace was built with 40-foot pilings made of poured concrete walls with rebar and steel cables. Why? One owner explained:

> At every point, from pilings to the roof and everything in between, when it came time to make a decision about what level of material or what to use, we didn't pay attention to code...We went above and beyond code, and we

asked the question: "What would survive the big one?"
And we consistently tried to build it for that.[5]

The Sand Palace is a perfect analogy for Matthew 7:24–27:

Therefore everyone who hears these words of mine and puts them into practice is like a wise man who built his house on the rock. The rain came down, the streams rose, and the winds blew and beat against that house; yet it did not fall, because it had its foundation on the rock. But everyone who hears these words of mine and does not put them into practice is like a foolish man who built his house on sand. The rain came down, the streams rose, the winds blew and beat against that house, and it fell with a great crash.

Perhaps there's something from both stories that we can take on our parenting journeys.

IT STARTS BEFORE BIRTH

Praying for your child should begin even before conception and continue during pregnancy. The perinatal nurse who oversees the Nurturing Your Newborn ministry at a church I attended repeatedly encourages the young mothers in her classes to pray out loud for their babies every single day, not only for the mental and physical health of both mother and infant, but also for the faith that child will grow to have. As a nurse and the mother of two God-loving young adults, she could testify about the importance of laying the foundation of faith even before that precious child is born.

---

5. Eric Levenson, "This home on Mexico Beach survived Hurricane Michael. That's no coincidence," *CNN*, October 16, 2018, www.cnn.com/2018/10/15/us/mexico-beach-house-hurricane-trnd/index.html.

God's Word tells us, "*You desired faithfulness **even in the womb;** you taught me wisdom in that secret place*" (Psalm 51:6). God told the prophet Jeremiah, "*Before I formed you in the womb I knew you, **before you were born** I set you apart*" (Jeremiah 1:5). The prophet Isaiah said, "*The Lord called me **from the womb**"* (Isaiah 49:1 ESV). King David, the man after God's own heart, acknowledged God from birth. (See 1 Samuel 13:14; Psalm 22:9). Timothy knew the Scriptures from the time he was an infant. (See 2 Timothy 3:15.)

The Lord was the anchor and hope for these amazing men's souls *from the beginning,* keeping them from drifting away. "*We have this hope as an anchor for the soul, firm and secure*" (Hebrews 6:19).

Children need a sturdy anchor, a solid foundation of truth, and the knowledge that these tools will keep them secure from turbulent winds and storms in times of trouble. The largest tree will fall if its roots (its anchors) are not deep enough to support it. Helical piles are deep-foundation elements (anchors) used to support buildings. The sturdiness and strength of a structure are only as solid as the foundation it rests upon. Shirley K. Morgenthaler says:

> Stone by stone, we set the foundation for the expectations of living—the traditions and values...The foundation must be laid before the walls or floors can be added...God has been the perfect Architect. His design has been flawless... the important is always worth doing, *right from the start...* Without that anchor, the unknown can be dreaded and feared. With the Holy Spirit as our mooring and foundation, the future is welcomed no matter what it holds.[6]

6. Dr. Shirley K. Morgenthaler, *Right from the Start: A Parent's Guide to the Young Child's Faith Development* (St. Louis, MO: Concordia Publishing House, 2001).

PREPARING THE FOUNDATION

My friend Chris's dad loved to garden. From the time his grandkids were toddlers, he taught them how to grow nutritious food to eat or beautiful flowers to touch and smell by planting seeds in the right soil. Chris says her two children delighted in helping Grandpa till and fertilize the ground, plant the seeds, water the garden, and eventually pick the vegetables and flowers.

Spiritually, the process is much the same. *Preparing the soil*—from the time children are in the womb to three years of age—is the first step in building a solid foundation to support their spiritual life. Without preparation, the foundation could become weak, giving the world a chance to dismantle or destroy what has been constructed.

Even if this spiritual work begins after the child's third birthday, the foundation can still be built upon good soil. Honestly, I wish I had discovered and applied many of the things that I learned in my research as I was raising my children. I did my best with what I knew, and God was faithful to call my children to Him. I thank God that He can restore whatever has been lost, as it's never too late to start transforming their hearts and minds. *"I will repay you for the years the locusts have eaten—the great locust and the young locust, the other locusts and the locust swarm—my great army that I sent among you"* (Joel 2:25).

If you didn't start early with your children, please don't feel guilty. How can you be guilty of not doing something you didn't know? God is able to bless your faithfulness whenever you obey what you have learned.

Nothing can prepare children for life lessons more effectively than the Word of God. I remember reading the story about Mack, a first-time father who took this truth to heart. As he was preparing the nursery for his unborn son, he wrote passages of Scripture on the walls before he painted them hunter green. These words of God's wisdom, love, and truth will surround Mack's son as he grows.

Just as the Sand Palace was built to withstand destructive elements, we want to raise our children to withstand the evil intentions of Satan, who comes only *"to steal and kill and destroy"* (John 10:10). We do this by adhering to the Word of God and seeking the guidance of His Holy Spirit.

2

IT'S ALWAYS THE RIGHT TIME

We are blessed today with an amazing amount of knowledge about the unborn child in the womb. Technology has far surpassed the fuzzy black-and-white ultrasound printouts from decades past. We can see that tiny baby's facial features so clearly that we can say, "He looks like his dad!" We can tell when their heartbeats begin, know when they are uncomfortable, and watch them hiccup or suck their thumb.

We know that unborn human babies can hear sounds eighteen weeks after conception. More amazingly, they can recognize the difference between two languages. Dr. Utako Minal, an associate professor of linguistics at the University of Kansas, and his team discovered that fetuses responded differently to the rhythm of language. Their tiny heartbeats changed when they heard an unfamiliar language, indicating that they recognized a rhythmical difference.[7]

I believe that Scripture acknowledges that unborn babies can hear. Luke 1:41–44 states:

When Elizabeth heard Mary's greeting, the baby leaped in her womb, and Elizabeth was filled with the Holy Spirit. In

---

7. Rick Hellman, "Study Shows Language Development Starts in the Womb," University of Kansas, July 18, 2017, news.ku.edu/2017/07/13/study-shows-language-development-starts-womb.

> *a loud voice, she exclaimed: "Blessed are you among women, and blessed is the child you will bear! But why am I so favored, that the mother of my Lord should come to me? As soon as the sound of your greeting reached my ears, the baby in my womb leaped for joy."*

A research team at the University of Wurzburg discovered that infants cry in the accents of their parents. Apparently, they were heavily influenced by the language they heard while still in the mother's womb.[8]

Unborn babies may also be able to glimpse the outside world! Findings from scientists at Lancaster University indicate that a fetus will turn its head toward shapes that resemble faces, but will ignore other objects. These findings, published in *Current Biology*, suggest that the fetus may recognize a human's face before birth and "has the capacity to process perceptual information."[9]

It is highly possible that singing songs and praying to Jesus out loud has a positive effect on an unborn baby. And you have a captive audience because your baby is not going to run away! So use this time to connect their heart and mind to Jesus.

PRAYING OVER CHILDREN

It's a privilege and a gift to pray over our children, asking God to protect and guide them. I always prayed words of prophecy, claiming that my children would follow Jesus all their lives. Again, our children are blessings, gifts, and great rewards, given to us by God for His glory.

---

8. Kathleen Wermke, quoted by Robert Emmerich, "Language begins with the very first cry," *Informationsdienst Wissenschaft* (The Science Information Service), May 11, 2009, idw-online.de/de/news342774.
9. Vincent M. Reid, et al., "The Human Fetus Preferentially Engages with Face-like Visual Stimuli," *Current Biology*, June 8, 2017, doi.org/10.1016/j.cub.2017.05.044.

A great way for pregnant moms to start a new prayer tradition is to ask baby shower guests to write specific prayers, requests, and blessings for their unborn child. These can all be kept in a journal and added to daily prayer time. What a privilege to pray over your little ones with help from special friends and family members!

Here is a sample prayer to pray before and after birth:

Thank You, Jesus, for giving me a great reward: a life created in Your lovely image. I know my child is a miracle destined by You before the foundations of the world were laid. Help me to pray the words given by Your Holy Spirit to claim my child's salvation.

May my child always be obedient to You, fulfilling Your will and purpose. Help me to teach (name) the ways of the Lord so (he/she) will never depart from You and Your love. I pray You will place a deep desire to know You and Your holy Word in (name's) heart and mind. Help (him/her) to be able to discern between good and evil and have only godly fear.

May (name) never grieve but always be overflowing with the Holy Spirit. I pray (he/she) will be Your devoted disciple all the days of (his/her) life. Fill (name) with Your peace, hope, and love. May (he/she) marry the person You handpick for (him/her), and may their children believe in You and worship You all the days of their lives. If Your best for them is to remain single, help them to be content and fulfilled.

May (name) have a pure heart and a gracious, loving, and kind character. May the fruit of Your Spirit dwell deeply and flow from (him/her) freely. Give (name) health, prosperity, and long life in service to You and to others. May (he/she) love as You love! In Jesus's name I pray, Amen.

GROWTH OF A CHILD'S MIND

I loved to hear my young children saying their prayers. It warmed my heart to hear them say, "I wuv You, Jesus." Did they really love Him? I think so.

Maybe you're wondering at what age children comprehend and grasp biblical truths. I believe this can occur in early childhood. From birth to age five, a child's brain develops more rapidly than at any other time in life. This is why they can learn multiple languages relatively early, learn to read, and much more.

From birth to two years old, children learn about the world through their senses and object manipulation. Piaget's Theory of Cognitive Development posits that learning comes from imitation, memory, and thought, moving from reflexes to thinking about actions and then actually performing those actions.[10] This is the time to teach them to say *yes* to you and *no* to themselves so that they develop self-control and self-discipline.[11]

From ages two to five, children develop memory and imagination, comprehend the meaning of symbols, and understand the concepts of past and future. Studies indicate that a toddler's brain is already 75 percent fully formed at age two. Dr. Shirley Morgenthaler explains:

> During the first three years of life, the young child develops more rapidly than any other period of time. The child's cognitive abilities virtually explode as new tasks are tried and mastered…Spiritual growth also takes place, or fails to take place, during these earliest years.[12]

10. Robert J. Keeley, *Helping Our Children Grow in Faith: How the Church Can Nurture the Spiritual Development of Kids* (Grand Rapids, MI: Baker Publishing Group, 2008), 101.
11. Reb Bradley, *Child Training Tips: What I Wish I Knew When My Children Were Young* (Washington, DC: WND Books, 2014), 51.
12. Morgenthaler, *Right from the Start*, 33.

About 90 percent of a child's brain has developed by age five. At this stage, besides comprehending language, they can show empathy and sympathy, making it probable that they can also grasp biblical truths. They are like sponges, soaking up every drop of information. Let's saturate them in the love and knowledge of God.

Have you ever said to yourself, "If only I had (fill in the blank) when my kids were younger"? I know I have—and so has my friend Ellen.

Ellen didn't become a Christian until her children were well into elementary school. As a result, she often struggles with the time she feels she lost in raising them to follow Christ. Lamenting this to her therapist one day, she was encouraged by the truth her counselor shared: "God's timeline is right on time. And in His kingdom, it's never too late to start." Thank God it's never too late to prepare our children to be equipped in His Word for any evil they may face.

It takes diligence to keep discouragement, distractions, guilt, and anger—the devil's tools—from sinking us into the spirit of inadequacy or regret. To counter this, we should fix our eyes on Jesus, *"the pioneer and perfecter of faith"* (Hebrews 12:2). He can restore what the locusts have eaten. (See Joel 2:25.)

I love this amazing story from Pastor Erwin W. Lutzer:

Years ago, archeologists found grain buried in the tombs of Egyptian Pharaohs. Incredibly, they grew when they planted the seeds and exposed them to water and sunshine! For some 4,000 years, these seeds gave no evidence of life, but under the right conditions, the dormant life grew.[13]

---

13. Erwin W. Lutzer, *How to Break a Stubborn Habit* (Eugene, OR: Harvest House Publishers, 2017), 78.

Let's get our tools ready and start planting the future harvest! Remember, we are instilling in our children the only imperishable seed, Jesus Christ, *"through the living and enduring word of God"* (1 Peter 1:23).

3

THE DIVINE
PARENTING MANUAL

When I was little, after my mother called me to breakfast, we would say our morning prayers and thank God for our food. I remember bowing my head and folding my hands as my mother would say a prayer. I'm so thankful for these times with her as I witnessed her faith.

I have a dear friend who is raising her great-grandchild. She has done something similar with him since his birth. As she rocked him to sleep when he was an infant, she would pray that the Lord would bless him to be a mighty and faithful God warrior. He is now eight years old, and she prays a nightly blessing over him that you can use with your own children:

Dear heavenly Father and Lord Jesus,

Thank You for this day. Thank You for watching over us, for providing everything we need, and for loving us again today.

Thank You for our whole family and bless each one: [list names of family members and pets too if you like]. Help us to love each other well.

Bless [child's name] in every way. Bless his/her mind, that s/he is smart, wise, and discerning. Bless his/her body, that s/he is healthy, strong, and athletic. Bless his/her heart, that s/he is kind, loving, and caring.

Please keep Your angels with [child's name] all day and all night, to protect and guide him/her. Remind [child's name] in his/her heart and mind how much You love him/her and that You will always be with him/her.

Help [child's name] have a good night's sleep tonight, with happy thoughts and godly dreams so s/he will have a great day tomorrow.

Help us to love You with all of our hearts. In Jesus's name, we pray. Amen.

My friend's prayers often include revelations from their Bible time together or what the Lord has revealed to her. She tells me that if anyone else puts him to bed, he insists on *the blessing* before going to sleep.

Do you have a specific prayer time? In the morning, I give thanks and praise to the Lord, pray to Him, and read my Bible. God's Word says, *"From the rising of the sun to the place where it sets, the name of the LORD is to be praised"* (Psalm 113:3). In addition to my request that I fulfill His will, I also pray, "Holy Spirit, please empty me of me and fill me with You. Let all my words, actions, deeds, and everything I say and do be all of You and none of me." When faced with a decision, if I forget to ask the Lord for guidance, I hope that prayer will cover it! I want to obey God in everything I do and say; prayer reminds me that I can't do anything without relying on His Holy Spirit to guide and direct me. Our children need to learn that as well.

IS PROVERBS 22:6 A GUARANTEE?

An often-quoted verse for raising godly children is Proverbs 22:6: *"Start children off in the way they should go, and even when they are old they will not turn from it.*" We wish to have our children become adult disciples of Jesus, so we train them up in the way they should go and disciple them in the Word. The author of Proverbs, King Solomon, was given godly wisdom, but it's best to understand that the proverbs are not absolute guarantees; they are conditioned by prevailing circumstances. The purpose of this book of the Bible is, "*To know wisdom and instruction, to understand words of insight, to receive instruction in wise dealing, in righteousness, justice, and equity; to give prudence to the simple, knowledge and discretion to the youth*" (Proverbs 1:2–4 ESV).

Proverbs 22:6 does not guarantee that our children will not depart from what they are taught. Only God knows who will receive salvation. That said, if children are raised in a strong, Bible-believing, righteous-living atmosphere, trained in the way of the Lord daily, they are more likely to stay strong in their faith.

Let us fit our little ones with the corrective lens of truth and the precise compass of the right direction, anchored in Jesus and His Word. We can use these tools against the evil one, who impairs spiritual forces to steer us and our children into sin and destruction. The thief comes to steal the very souls of our children, for he knows they are the future that will promote either a godly kingdom or an evil one here on earth.

THE MOST IMPORTANT PARENTAL COMMAND

Have you ever wondered what is the most important prayer or Bible verse for giving direction and guidance to parents? Many theologians believe it is the *Shema* (shuh-mah) prayer, rooted in Deuteronomy 6:4–9 and reframed in Deuteronomy 11:13–21. It is considered to be the most essential prayer for the Jewish people. They are commanded to pray it twice a day, and it must permeate all areas of their lives, prompting them to love God with all of their being and teach their children to do the same.

In Deuteronomy 6:1, Moses tells the Israelites that the Lord wants them to obey the commands, decrees, and laws that He has provided and teach them to their children. Moses explains, *"Be careful to obey so that it may go well with you and that you may increase greatly in a land flowing with milk and honey, just as the LORD, the God of your ancestors, promised you"* (Deuteronomy 6:3).

Moses then shares the Lord's commands: *"Hear, O Israel: The LORD our God, the LORD is one. Love the LORD your God with all your heart and with all your soul and with all your strength. These commandments...are to be on your hearts. **Impress them on your children**...when you **sit at home** and when you **walk along the road**, when you **lie down** and when you **get up**"* (Deuteronomy 6:4–7).

What a gift it is to have these words to guide us as followers of Christ today. God tells us to impress His commandments upon our children *all day long! Impressing* means to disciple, impact, influence, lead, love, and mold. God's Word is the right tool to help our children gain a lifelong, loving relationship with Him that will hopefully keep them strong as they face the ever-increasing anti-Christian, secular society.

THE SHEMA PRAYER

The word *Shema* means "to listen, to obey." There is a difference between listening and hearing. We can *hear* many things, like wind blowing through the trees, birds chirping early in the morning, or the noise of city traffic. However, listening is an active discipline. Failing to listen to God's directives may lead to sin and deter one from living a robust Christian life. Throughout the Bible, God and His Son Jesus repetitively command that we instruct our children in the ways of the Lord. This teaching is a command that preserves life, sets God's people apart as holy and saved, and ensures the preservation of God's covenant for all future generations.

If you visit a Jewish home, you will see a tiny box called a *mezuzah* hanging next to the door frame. This box contains a tightly wound scroll upon which is written the *Shema* prayer. It is a symbol to remind the family of our glorious God and His commands.

When one of the Jewish teachers of the law asked Jesus which commandment was the most important, the Lord quoted from the Shema:

> "The most important one," answered Jesus, "is this: 'Hear, O Israel: The Lord our God, the Lord is one.' Love the Lord your God with all your heart and with all your soul and with all your mind and with all your strength.'" (Mark 12:29–30)

Jesus added a word. It's subtle, but it emphasizes the term *strength*, and any Jewish teacher would have noticed it. Did you catch it? It's the word *mind*. Pastor Bobby Schuller notes:

> In doing so, [Jesus] made a beautiful rhetorical point about the mind. He was saying, "Your strength is in your mind." In the eyes of Rabbi Jesus, loving God with your strength is the same as loving him with your mind...The strength to do what you need to do begins in your mind.[14]

Another word that stands out is *all*. The word *all* means whole, entire, total, including everything without exception. Both the Old Testament *Shema* that Moses penned and Jesus's words underscore a point we might find difficult to grasp. How can one love God with *all* their heart, *all* their soul, *all* their mind, and *all* their strength? This can only be accomplished through Christ Jesus. Repetitively praying the *Shema* helps to imprint these instructional directives on our minds for retention and recall, which results in obedient

---

14. Bobby Schuller, *Change Your Thoughts, Change Your World: How Life-Giving Thoughts Can Unlock Your Destiny* (Nashville, TN: Nelson Books, 2019), 134–135.

action and proper worship toward God the Father, God the Son, and God the Holy Spirit and teaching our children to follow suit.

There are many books and blogs that share ideas for teaching little ones what the Ten Commandments are or how to understand the Lord's Prayer. Your child's age will determine which method will be the most comprehensible to them. Here are some tips that helped my family.

THE TEN COMMANDMENTS

What do you do daily to remind yourself and your household to love and adhere to the commandments of God? Elisabeth painted a wall in her children's playroom with chalkboard paint so they could write verses they are working to memorize directly on the wall. Each month, they begin with a new verse, and they spend the next four weeks memorizing it, talking about what it means to them, and sharing it with others.

When it comes to learning, children are best served by repetition. Learning the Ten Commandments, accompanied by action, will help transform their hearts and reinforce the teaching of the biblical principles we hope to instill.

Here is a simplified version of the Ten Commandments: 1. Always put God first; 2. No pretend gods; there is only one God; 3. Respect God's name; don't say it when you aren't talking to or about Him; 4. Respect God's day of rest; it's a day to relax, worship God, and think about who He is; 5. Respect your parents because God says so; 6. Don't kill (or hurt) people; 7. Respect marriage because God tells you to; 8. Never steal; 9. Never lie; 10. Don't be jealous; God is taking care of you.

THE LORD'S PRAYER

As a child, I was taught to memorize the Lord's Prayer. I remember how happy I was the first time I recited it from memory.

The Lord's Prayer is also a call to honor God and live according to His heavenly ways. Jesus gave us this prayer as the perfect example of how we should pray:

> *Our Father in heaven, hallowed be your name, your kingdom come, your will be done, on earth as it is in heaven. Give us today our daily bread. And forgive us our debts, as we also have forgiven our debtors. And lead us not into temptation but deliver us from the evil one.* (Matthew 6:9–13)

Here is the Lord's Prayer for little ones: Dear God our Father who lives in heaven, Your name is powerful. Help us to do what You want on earth like what You want is done by everyone in heaven. Please give us all we need today. Forgive us when we do wrong and help us to forgive people who do wrong to us. Help us to make good choices and protect us from everything bad or evil. Help us do everything for You so others will know we love You. Amen.

MEDITATION AND HEART TRANSFORMATION

God loves us so much that He provides what we need to help transform our hard hearts into hearts that not only love Him but also extend love to others. He is the perfect heart transplant physician! God reminded Israel, *"These commandments that I give you today are to be on your hearts"* (Deuteronomy 6:6); we are to meditate on His precepts and consider His ways. (See Psalm 119:15.) His Word gives us the best way to adhere to these commandments: *"Bind them always on your heart; fasten them around your neck. When you walk, they will guide you; when you sleep, they will watch over you; when you awake, they will speak to you"* (Proverbs 6:21–22).

Schuller points out, "The Bible says to 'study' the Scripture only four times, while it says to 'meditate' on Scripture eighteen times."[15] Studying educates us, while meditation helps to keep our minds focused on the living Word that transforms us to be like Christ.

The heart contains our desires and directs our individual choices. The Hebrew people believed that the *heart* encompassed a person's entire personality, including their intellect, emotions, and will.[16]

Moses knew that the hearts of Israel's adults had to be right before they could teach their children. He told them, *"Take to* **heart** *all the words I have solemnly declared to you this day, so that you may command your children to obey carefully all the words of this law. They are not just idle words for you—they are your* **life**" (Deuteronomy 32:46–47).

We all love rewards, especially from our heavenly Father, and there is a wonderful promise for those who obey. After Moses died, the Lord told Joshua, *"Keep this Book of the Law always on your lips; meditate on it day and night, so that you may be careful to do everything written in it.* **Then you will be prosperous and successful**" (Joshua 1:8). We hope in the Lord that we and our children will be prosperous and successful in fulfilling the call to preach the good news, stand strong in faith, and make disciples, always obedient to the Lord until He calls us home.

> *But from everlasting to everlasting the* Lord's *love is with those who fear him, and his righteousness with their children's children—with those who keep his covenant and remember to obey his precepts.* (Psalm 103:17–18)

---

15. Schuller, *Change Your Thoughts, Change Your World*, 11.
16. Dr. Howard Hendricks, *Teaching to Change Lives: Seven Proven Ways to Make Your Teaching Come Alive* (New York, NY: Multnomah, 1987), 85.

TELL THE NEXT GENERATION

God commands us to teach the next generation. Here are two examples:

> *My people, hear my teaching; listen to the words of my mouth...we will* **tell the next generation**...*to teach their children...even the children yet to be born, and they in turn would* **tell their children.** (Psalm 78:1, 4–6)

> *Great is the* LORD *and most worthy of praise; his greatness no one can fathom.* **One generation commends your works to another;** *they tell of your mighty acts. They speak of the glorious splendor of your majesty—and I will meditate on your wonderful works. They tell of the power of your awesome works—and I will proclaim your great deeds. They celebrate your abundant goodness and joyfully sing of your righteousness.* (Psalm 145:3–7)

ALLEGIANCE TO GOD ALONE

Many sports fans have a passionate allegiance to their favorite teams. My friend's nephew is a *cheesehead.* "Go Packers!" is not just a cheer for this guy; it is a passionate football season tradition that comes with its own set of rituals and expectations—so much so that he has painted the inside of his garage, including the floor, with the Green Bay Packers' colors of green, gold, and white. Game day means wearing a Packers jersey and foam cheese hat and eating cheese cracker snacks, cheese pizza, and cheesy popcorn. He never misses a single minute of pre-game analysis, game-play, and post-game interviews. And he has passed this tradition down to his son and daughter, who faithfully watch every Packers game with him each season.

Wouldn't it be wonderful if all of God's people showed that same allegiance and dedication to God that many sports fans demonstrate? God desires that kind of love and dedication. In addition to other wonderful biblical commands, the *Shema* prayer requires allegiance to God alone and requires parents to pass this allegiance on to their children. This prayer/command upholds the *very first* commandment written by the finger of God: "*You shall have no other gods before me*" (Exodus 20:3).

By demonstrating our love and devotion to the one true God and His commands, our children will see that it truly is our heart's desire that they emulate us. Nothing is more important or beneficial than intentionally and devotionally loving the Father, the Son, and the Holy Spirit. Let's celebrate this love and devotion with our children because we are a part of the ultimate winning team!

But before we can guide, direct, and raise our children with godly wisdom, we must prepare their hearts and minds to be receptive and willing—in other words, teach them how to be obedient. Yes, kids can act like wild animals sometimes. We have to tame them before we can train them.

4

MAKING OBEDIENCE EASIER THROUGH DISCIPLINE

Disciplining children is so much fun, right? Uh, no way! Especially if you have a strong-willed, independent child. My daughter threw temper tantrums every time I told her, "No candy before dinner," or "You have to put your shoes on before you go outside." She would yell, "No! I don't want to!" She didn't want to obey me.

So how can we teach our children to be obedient? Isn't that the million-dollar question? And how does the discipline we apply help our children to become disciples later? I think it is best to understand that discipline has much to do with instructing them in wisdom. We can discipline them by providing them with knowledge, train them by developing proficiencies, and correct them by taking action to alter unwanted behaviors. God's Word says wisdom is key. "*The beginning of wisdom is this: Get wisdom. Though it cost all you have, get understanding*" (Proverbs 4:7).

MANY PARENTS HATE TO DISCIPLINE

I really hated those moments when I had to discipline my kids. It would break my heart to see the tears streaming down their faces when they faced the consequences of their misbehavior. Maybe you too feel this way when you discipline your children, and that old saying, "This hurts me more than it hurts you" is very real for you.

However, withholding discipline can be detrimental to children as they grow. The Bible says that King David never rebuked his sons; he became angry at their actions but did nothing—to the detriment of himself and his sons. (See 2 Samuel 13–15.) King David was not a perfect parent, but he knew perfectly well that he needed to be obedient to the commands of the Lord. His sins of omission hurt his sons Amnon, Absalom, and Adonijah, and he did not set a good example for his children regarding how to raise the next generation.

We need to be obedient while also understanding that there is grace in all we do. Parenting takes patience and practice; practice does not mean we will be perfect. We are *parenting practitioners!*

It's sad to realize that some children grow up believing that a lack of discipline proves their parents did not love or care for them. Studies show that children recognize that their parents' loving discipline is meant to help them become better people. Children also understand they are disciplined out of love, and this instruction through discipline is a connection with their parents' Christian beliefs.

Mason was what some would call a *mouthy child*, even before kindergarten. If his mother told him to pick up his toys or feed the dog, or he was being disciplined, Mason would respond with back talk. Some children do this to see how much power they have or to test their independence. But children who consistently talk back to their parents or make sassy remarks may become adults who cannot take directives or have self-control in conversations. Discipline is an act of love from the Lord to us and from us to our children. Proverbs 3:11–12 says:

> My son, do not despise the LORD's discipline, and do not resent his rebuke, because the LORD disciplines those he loves, as a father the son he delights in.

If we desire to be obedient to the directive to *"go and make disciples of all nations, baptizing them in the name of the Father and of the Son and of the Holy Spirit"* (Matthew 28:19), then disciplining our children is a necessity. The word *discipline* means to train or instruct. It comes from the root word *disciple*, which in turn comes from the Latin word *discipulus*, meaning *student*.

It's important to recognize that discipline never means physical punishment. Proverbs 12:1 tells us, *"Whoever loves discipline loves knowledge, but whoever hates correction is stupid."* This proverb would be illogical if discipline referred to physical punishment, for then it would read, "Whoever loves physical punishment loves knowledge."[17] As parents, we know that loving, godly discipline brings knowledge and transformation. Jesus gave instruction to His disciples and continues to instruct us through His Word and the Holy Spirit.

Perhaps you've noticed the resemblance between the words *discipline* and *discipling*? The "e" or "g" at the end of each word are the only letters differentiating between the two. Jesus disciplined His followers so they could become effective disciples. This chapter thoroughly examines the importance of lovingly disciplining our children so they can become effective disciples of Jesus and virtuous citizens in the world. Isn't that what we all desire to be?

PROPER DISCIPLINE TRANSFORMS A SELFISH HEART.

LACK OF DISCIPLINE IS COSTLY

One of the greatest challenges facing parents today is technology—specifically, cell phones, computers, and tablets. Even when young children don't have access to their own electronic

---

17. Angela Harders, *Gospel-Based Parenting: A Biblical Study on Discipline and Discipling* (Unicorn Publishing Group, 2019), 69.

devices, they are exposed to all forms of technology at an early age. Certainly, most parents are cognizant of the online dangers children face today. But, sadly, many are unaware of—or choose to ignore—the impact too much screen time can have on their children's emotions as they grow older. Unrestricted or minimally restricted access to electronic media can lead to social and emotional struggles by the time children reach their preteen and teen years. Limiting their access to technology is one way we can discipline our children.

Lack of appropriate discipline can lead to pride instead of humility and unbelief instead of faith. Kids who are constantly on their phones, for example, may seek their glory instead of God's glory, rely on their power instead of His power, covet their goodness instead of His goodness, and demonstrate self-centered actions instead of self-sacrificial ones.

As parents, we are to be our children's compasses, walking beside them and pointing them in the right direction. If we don't, the world will happily lead them in the wrong direction! Without discipline, children can grow up to become egotistical, bombastic, self-absorbed, narcissistic, prideful, and strong-willed. Prisons are full of people who perhaps lacked discipline as children and were not guided correctly.

GUILT VERSES SHAME

When I was a little girl, my mother would take me to the local store down the road from our house. One day, I decided to take a pack of gum and put it in my pocket, even though I knew it was wrong. After we left the store, I took the gum out of my pocket. My mother marched me back into the store to return the gum and apologize. She never said, "Shame on you."

It is important to note that there is a difference between guilt and shame. Guilt tells children that they did something wrong, and they hopefully will not do it again. Shame can make children believe they are *bad*, *stupid*, or *dumb*. Parents who cause their children to feel ashamed can lead them to believe they will never measure up and this feeling might push them to believe they are worthless.

God's Word gives us examples that show the difference between shame and guilt among the apostles. After Judas betrayed Jesus, he felt shame; "*he was seized with remorse*" and "*hanged himself.*" (Matthew 27:3, 5.) Peter, after denying Christ three times, felt so guilty that "*he went outside and wept bitterly*" (Matthew 26:75).

According to the National Social Anxiety Center, "social anxiety disorder typically stems from distorted, negative, shame-based beliefs about ourselves."[18] Shame is a result of critical assessment from others and against oneself. People who live with shame often feel anxious or worthless. The neuropsychologist Dr. Michelle Bengtson says, "Worry, anxiety, and fear are considered the common cold of mental illness and are a direct path to losing our peace."[19] We don't want our children to feel the anxiety or worthlessness that often accompanies feelings of shame.

LITTLE EYES ARE WATCHING

Children love to watch what their parents are doing. Young children correlate their view of God with what they see modeled by their parents. It's adorable to see your little ones be the first to bow their heads and fold their tiny hands in prayer before dinner because they see you do the same thing daily.

One day, as I was sitting on the couch reading my Bible, my little daughter brought out one of her picture books. She sat on the couch

---

18. Larry Cohen, "Shame: The Oft-Neglected Ingredient in Social Anxiety," December 22, 2022, National Social Anxiety Center, nationalsocialanxietycenter. com/2022/12/22/shame-oft-neglected-ingredient-in-social-anxiety.
19. Dr. Michelle Bengtson, *Breaking Anxiety's Grip: How to Reclaim the Peace God Promises* (Grand Rapids, MI: Revell, 2019), 19.

next to me and said, "See, Mommy, I weed my Bible too!" It was during this sweet, loving moment that I thought, "I better get her a children's Bible." Studies have shown that a positive, close relationship between parents and children is connected to their perception of a loving and forgiving God. This reinforces that we are made in His image and should reflect it daily in all we do and say.

Since little eyes are always watching, we shouldn't make a judgment call based on our anxiety or irritation level, which is something I have done. We wear many hats as adults, and our list of responsibilities and commitments can often get the best of us. In those moments when we are tired or stressed, it can be too easy to respond in anger or frustration when our children misbehave or defy us. It's best to make sure we are in control of our emotions before we address our child's behavior.

When we do lose our temper and become unreasonably frustrated with our children, we need to regroup and then offer a genuine apology to them. Without that, we can easily lose some of the ground we have gained in our parenting and discipline in love.

If we want to raise our children to be spiritually strong in Jesus, like a mighty oak tree with deep roots, we need to be consistent in our discipline and steadfast in our convictions to help transform their hearts. Heart transformation is of vital importance for us and for them as it ultimately determines one's actions.

Dr. Scott Turansky, cofounder of the National Center for Biblical Parenting, says:

> When experience, teaching, and values need to be integrated into our lives, it happens in the workshop of our hearts. Information comes into our heads constantly, but much of it just stays there. Only what moves into our hearts becomes part of our lives.[20]

---

20. Dr. Scott Turansky and Joanne Miller, *Parenting Is Heart Work* (Colorado Springs, CO: David C. Cook, 2005), 28.

The Holy Spirit continuously transforms us and our children. Thank God for that! Those who are saved call this *sanctification*. We may find ourselves saying the same thing a hundred times to our children. And when we become exasperated as we struggle to do what we know is right, it's important to remember that our children are watching.

GOD'S GRACE AND MERCY

I can't count the number of times I felt like Paul when he cried out, *"For what I want to do I do not do, but what I hate I do"* (Romans 7:15). I've always wanted to be the very best parent and do everything right, but I wasn't, I didn't, and I still don't. Thankfully, the Lord is patient and loving and extends His grace toward His children, giving us an example to follow for our own children. The apostle Paul ended most of his letters with a prayer that God's grace would be with the recipients.

God extends both grace and mercy to us. Grace is God's unmerited favor toward us, while mercy is His compassion and kindness toward us when we are sinful and deserve His just wrath. It is by God's grace that we are given the wisdom we need to raise our children properly and show mercy when they sin. Grace transforms parenting, makes mercy paramount, and magnifies the Lord's great love for us and our children.

It really is simple to infuse grace into how we discipline our children. After any consequence is doled out, make it a point to sit down with the child who made the mistake or broke the rule. Lovingly look them in the eye and remind them of what remains true: "You are my child. I will always love you, even when you are disobedient. Because of that, there is always another chance to try again. I believe you can and will do better next time." Those simple words will remind your child that grace is always a part of love and discipline. They will be encouraged to do better in the future.

LEARNING SELF-CONTROL

One day, my daughter walked into the kitchen as I said, "Get behind me, Satan!" to a lonely cupcake on the counter. She asked me who I was talking to, and I told her, "That cupcake. I already ate two!" We laughed, but I was serious—I needed self-control against that evil cupcake! Learning self-control is a lifelong process.

Parenting doesn't end when your child becomes an adult. I still offer advice to my adult children before they ask. My son will say, "Thanks for your advice, Mom, but I just want you to hear my concern. I don't need you to fix anything." It is so hard to turn off the mom-to-the-rescue button. It's also best to be a proactive parent, trying to be prepared to handle various situations, versus a reactive parent, who acts on impulse.

For example, instead of issuing a timeout, give your children a break. Dr. Scott Turansky states, "Time out is a sentence given to a child for crime committed, and you are like the policeman keeping him there. A break is a refreshing new approach."[21] Lovingly telling children to take a break and come back when they are ready to discuss the situation affords them sufficient time to think about what they did and what they could or should have done differently. This can encourage them to have self-control, think before they act or react, and become critical thinkers. This gentler parenting technique also strengthens the connection between child and parent.

We want to encourage a heart change, not just a behavioral change. A changed heart is a repentant heart. Again, it is essential to impart discipline with loving guidance. I remember the tender moments when I held my children in my arms, wiping away tears as they said, "I'm sorry."

---

21. Dr. Scott Turansky and Joanne Miller, *Parenting Is Heart Work: Training Manual* (Lawrenceville, NJ: National Center for Biblical Training, 2015), 57.

The ultimate goal of discipline should be helping our children become self-controlled and self-motivated toward right action. Motivation to serve others should come from a desire to love others and Jesus, and self-motivation is something a child is taught and then applied *by the child*. If parents continue to remind their children of the things they should be doing, they rob them of the opportunity to learn how to become self-disciplined and self-motivated. Many want to raise their children to have self-esteem, but this often revolves around a self-centered approach based on personal abilities, achievements, or looks. It's better to guide children toward a biblical self-love that is paired with self-control and respect, which they can then extend to others.

Self-discipline teaches children to be respectful, have good manners, resist unhealthy or dangerous temptations, be patient, delay instant gratification, have self-control, and so much more. They also learn to become diligent in their work habits, even if they do not *feel* like continuing.

BOUNDARIES

It's also important to set boundaries, while also making sure that these do not become walls that divide us from our children. Boundaries can be negotiated or firm as long as they are established and understood. These can include limiting TV time, setting bedtime, making sure homework is done before playing, and similar parameters. Sometimes, these boundaries are established so we can protect our children from danger. I'm sure you've heard the phrase, "Nothing good happens after midnight." When my children were teenagers, I told them this to help them understand why I set a curfew. Boundaries promote a sense of security, build self-discipline, and teach respect for others' personal space, opinions, and belongings.

As a child, I was firmly told not to touch my mother's figurines, which were handmade by her loving sister. My mother was concerned that I might accidentally break these figurines, but when she told me I could not touch them, I wanted to touch them even more. Isn't that how kids are? Boundaries help us and our children understand our roles, responsibilities, and the consequences of poor decisions.

DEPENDABILITY AND CONSISTENCY MATTER

When it comes to discipline, consistency is key. If you say you're going to take something away from them or deliver a consequence, you must follow through with it. Even when it's difficult, even if you hate it, even when it would be easier to give in, you have to be consistent. And goodness, that is hard!

I could always depend on my mother to consistently correct any wayward behavior I exhibited. She did not let things slide by; she addressed the situation immediately. Consistency does not mean repetitive warnings. Constantly reminding our children to clean up their rooms, for example, teaches them that our first command is merely a suggestion. Then after several suggestions, we become angry with our child when the blame is on us for not being consistent in our discipline.

Being a loving parent who disciplines immediately sends the message to our children that they are worth the effort. They know and can depend on the fact that we say what we mean and mean what we say.

Behavior modification—such as giving a reward for good behavior—can work in some cases, such as potty training a child. But as children get older, we need to change their hearts instead so that they choose to do what is right.

You want your child to obey because it is the right thing to do, not because they will avoid punishment or receive a reward.

NATURAL, LOGICAL, AND CONTRIVED CONSEQUENCES

Children also learn well from the natural consequences of their actions. This affords some great life lessons, and I believe these types of consequences become ingrained in their minds. It certainly did for me. Although my mother told me not to touch the stove when it was hot, one day, I didn't listen, I got burned, and I cried. She did not scold me; she simply said, "You need to listen to me. I love you, and I want to protect you." I knew never to touch the stove again, but more importantly, I knew she was right, and that I would be wise to obey her instructions. I remember the incident lovingly. If she had yelled, spanked, or punished, I may have interpreted that as a lack of love rather than a lesson to wisely obey.

Another perfect example of a natural consequence was when my cousin's daughter jumped into the pool backward after being repeatedly told not to do that. She did not listen, jumped in, and smashed her open mouth on the swimming pool wall, shoving her upper teeth into her gums. Thankfully, the dentist told her parents that her teeth would eventually move back down. They did, and she never jumped backward into the pool again. The natural results of disobedience can be an effective deterrent. It's also helpful to discuss the negative consequences of a child's actions or poor choices afterward.

Logical consequences are predetermined by the parent. The goal is to teach a lesson that disobedience has consequences. For example, if Mason is told to put his toys away before he eats dinner and doesn't do so, he loses toy privileges the next day. Or if Melissa is told to get off her cell phone and finish her homework but doesn't, she loses the privilege of using her phone for a week.

Be aware of contrived consequences. For example, don't say, "No cake tonight" for something a child did earlier in the day that had nothing to do with cake. The discipline should be directly related to the undesired behavior so that the child will connect the consequences with their specific disobedient act.

During the Christmas season, I would hide Christmas presents in my bedroom closet, and my son knew he was not allowed to go in there before the holidays. One year, he didn't obey and found some of the presents I had bought him. He came running into the kitchen and excitedly exclaimed, "You got me a new Power Ranger!" I can't remember much about the toy, but I do remember the look on his face when he saw how disappointed I was. My sorrow, a natural consequence, was easy to see and sometimes served as a good deterrent against future misbehavior.

Positive reinforcement, acknowledging good behavior, and exhibiting love and faith encourage the desired behavior; negative comments, threats, or punishment do not. Proverbs 12:25 says, *"Anxiety weighs down the heart, but a kind word cheers it up."* For example, tell your child, "Hurry and put on your pajamas so we will have time for a bedtime story," rather than, "If you don't put on your pajamas, I won't read you a bedtime story." Telling kids that they did a great job getting ready for bed—by brushing their teeth and putting their things away, for example—will motivate them to continue this practice. And when you explain what they did to warrant being told "good job," they will remember to do it again.

For older children who are driving, you can say, "Remember to drive within the speed limit. I want you to come home safe and sound," instead of, "Don't speed because you'll get a ticket and lose the privilege of using the car." Even if both are true, people tend to respond better to positive reinforcement than negative comments.

I recall a fifth-grade student who was often disruptive during class because he didn't want to attend Sunday school. Instead of focusing on his rude behavior, I focused on him and offered positive reinforcement. When he sarcastically stated, "I'm not sure God exists," I replied, "Well, Jeff, I can see that you are a very smart boy and a natural leader. I hope you will continue to learn so you will come to a different conclusion."

During our time together, I called on him to pass out papers, assist me whenever help was needed, and often asked his opinion during class discussions. As a result, his behavior in class began to change. He was no longer disruptive but became actively involved, with a willingness to learn. His grandmother, who was raising him, told me he was a changed boy who was more respectful at home.

On the last day of class, Jeff waited to be the last student in line to say goodbye to me. As we hugged, he whispered in my ear, "Please pray for me." I reassured him that I would never forget him, and I would keep him in my prayers.

I learned what God could do through me when I allowed His loving Spirit to guide me. Instead of being led by my impulsive, sinful flesh that wanted me to react angrily each time Jeff tested me, I chose to exhibit grace. That disruptive, unbelieving, rude young boy changed me, too, for the better. As I empowered him to become a follower of Christ, I became a better teacher, one who emulated the love and grace of God that changes students.

SO EMBARRASSING!

To this day, I still vividly recall an incident that occurred when I was fifteen years old. The teenagers in my neighborhood used to meet at the local pizza place to socialize. I was allowed to go with my friends but had to be home before dark. This was a time when kids could walk home alone safely, and we lived right down the street from the pizzeria. One evening while out having fun with my friends, I thought walking home in the dark would be okay because I would be only a few minutes late. Well, I was wrong. My very consistent mother showed up, calling my name and practically blinding my friends with her flashlight as they stood next to their sports cars in the parking lot. Oh my, how embarrassing! You can imagine the situation if you know the wrath of an angry Italian mother. It took me two weeks before I could face my friends. I thought that surely they would have forgotten the incident by then. But they didn't, and for many years, it was a funny story everyone loved to retell.

I learned not to be late, for sure. But as a parent, I learned to never discipline my children in a way that would publicly embarrass them. Children should learn that rules are established because their parents love them, and when they disobey the rules, they will be loved and treated respectfully. Also, children should never feel that their parents love them because they obey their rules. That is conditional love, and we are called to love unconditionally.

LOVING BUT FIRM

Jesus used discipline tactics to set a standard of truth and explain hard-to-understand concepts; He nurtured and admonished when necessary. Likewise, firmness and kindness should be used together when disciplining a child because both are beneficial. Firmness demonstrates the importance of the situation at hand, and kindness shows love for the child.

My friend Sandra caught her young son constantly sneaking toys and other items into his backpack to take to school after she had explicitly asked him to leave them at home. These were not harmful or dangerous items, but action figures and Legos that he wanted to play with at school. Sandra repeatedly told her little boy that he might lose these things or get into trouble for playing with them in class. Again and again, she found the items at the bottom of his backpack under his schoolwork and notebooks. After catching him once again with his toys, Sandra removed them from his backpack. One by one, she put them inside a plastic bin that he could not have for two weeks. She then kindly but firmly explained to her son that this was the consequence of his disobedience. He hung his head, shed a couple of tears, and then said, "I know, Mommy. I am sorry." She was firm but kind, which made the difference in how he accepted her discipline.

CONSEQUENTIAL/CORRECTIVE DISCIPLINE

When I was a child, if I left my clothes on the floor and didn't put them in the laundry hamper, they didn't get washed. Getting ready for school one day, I was looking for a particular pair of pants, which I found lying on my floor—wrinkled and unwashed. In fact, a lot of my clothes were on the floor. I was so upset...but I learned that if I wanted clean clothes, I needed to use the hamper. My mother taught me that clothes would not be washed unless they were in the laundry hamper. This is a type of *consequential* discipline in which our actions lead to consequences.

Corrective discipline helps to correct wrong behavior. For example, Sage is messy by nature. She's notorious in her family for never leaving a space the way she found it. So if she left her bathroom a mess, her parents sent her back to the bathroom to clean it up. If she left the kitchen a mess, she had to close every cabinet, clean up every dish, and turn off every light before moving on to the next part of her day. If her clothes were scattered around her room, she had to pick them up, put them away, and wash what was dirty on her own. These simple lessons in corrective discipline will go a long way in helping Sage take ownership and responsibility as she grows up.

If your child steals something or borrows something and never returns it, they should return the item and offer something else in addition to it. According to God's Word, when we steal something, we are to pay the person back sevenfold. (See Proverbs 6:31.) Doing this is a more effective consequence than just giving back the item. For example, if a child purposely keeps a toy that does not belong to him, he should return the toy *and* offer something of value to his playmate. The consequence is that he now loses a toy.

EVERYONE ARGUES

We all argue from time to time because we feel our points are valid or correct. Children may argue over things that might not seem important to us but are important to them. When my son was four and my daughter was two, I remember walking into his room to see an angry look on his face and my daughter in tears. When I asked why he was angry and why she was crying, he said definitively that his toy car was faster than her toy car. I tried to keep a serious face because, for them, this was a serious issue. Because of their ages, I told them that they both have the right to think their car was faster, and then I distracted them from the situation by leading them out to the kitchen to help me bake cookies.

For older children, ask each child separately how they think they might've contributed to cause the argument or disagreement. Explain to them that God says we are to take the obstacle out of our own eyes before we instruct others. (See Matthew 7:3–5.) Afterward, have them look each other in the eyes and tell each other what they like about each other and why they love each other. Sometimes they will start laughing, which defuses the anger. Have them ask for forgiveness from each other, no matter who is right or wrong.

Share this Scripture with them:

> *So if you are offering your gift at the altar and there remember that your brother has something against you, leave your gift there before the altar and go. First be reconciled to your brother, and then come and offer your gift.*
>
> (Matthew 5:23–24 esv)

Notice it says if "*your brother* has something against you." It doesn't say you have sinned against your brother, only that your brother feels that you have done wrong toward him. This process of reconciliation will foster good feelings toward each other and teach your children to become others-centered.

STRONG-WILLED TODDLERS

No is a toddler's favorite word. These lovely little ones have learned the power of independence. Parents might laugh when the first *no* comes out of their toddler's mouth, but after hearing it repeatedly, it's not so cute anymore. Toddlers want and need to be individuals, but their means of expression should be allowed in a measured and protected environment that calls for loving disciplinary actions—when appropriate. Self-centered toddlers need the discipline of conversion. Oh, those little faces, so adorable when they're sleeping, can turn into *I mean business!* scowls when they want their way and expect you to accommodate them.

Toddlers naturally want to explore their world. As they take their baths, they may throw out more water than you care to wipe up off the floor. When bath time ends, crying may ensue because they don't want to stop. Tell your little one, "I know you are mad. You love to splash and have fun in the tub. Tomorrow we will have fun in the tub again." Empathy is an effective tool to defuse an angry outburst for all ages. Acknowledging their emotions and offering solutions can help greatly. It takes time, love, patience, and, most of all, consistency to help change the hearts and wills of children.

LEARNING TO SHARE

How many times have you seen a toddler who doesn't want to share? Ugh, almost all the time, right? Telling a three-year-old he cannot play with a toy unless he can share it with his friend is a valuable lesson that should be learned early. When children are very young, they often play side by side without interacting. When one child grabs a toy out of another child's hand, sometimes the child who loses the toy is complacent. But some children may react with a full-blown tantrum, which can be very disconcerting and deafening to our ears!

What can you do? One way to handle this situation is to take possession of the toy and say, "Okay, we all love this toy; it's a very nice toy. Can you share your toy for one minute with your friend?" Then ask the friend, "Will you give this toy back after your turn is finished? It's his toy, and he is being nice to share it with you." Then tell them both, "If you both cannot share this toy, no one can play with it. Jesus wants both of you to share."

Now, I know this doesn't always work the first time, and there might be a few temper tantrums, but after losing the privilege of playing with the toy a few times, they will understand that Mom means business.

This solution emphasizes two truths about Jesus: He has given us nice things, and He wants us to share His gifts with others. It's easier when children understand the difference between owning and sharing. Once children fully understand that the toy belongs to them and they are only sharing it, they may become more compliant with the request that they share. If they will not share, loss of playing with the toy is an appropriate consequence.

A good way to teach the concepts of sharing and patience is to have children sit in a circle while you bring out a new toy for them to pass around. Each child gets to play with the toy until a timer buzzes, when it's passed on to the next child. Have each child talk about the new toy and what they like about it. Tell them that if they all share nicely with each other, everyone will get a fun snack.

Learning to wait patiently while taking turns is an important virtue for adults too. We take turns waiting in line at the store, driving in traffic, waiting for food at a restaurant, and in many other situations. *How* we wait displays our character. We want our children to see us waiting calmly so that we are good role models for them. Patience also reduces stress levels.

RECOGNIZING PROBLEMATIC DISCIPLINING APPROACHES

WHAT ARE WE COMMUNICATING TO OUR CHILDREN?

In computer science, there is a saying, "Garbage in, garbage out." It highlights the idea that the quality of the data fed into a computer directly affects the quality of the output. I believe the same is true of one of my favorite sayings about the "data" we feed our children: "Wisdom in, wisdom out."

We must be careful of what we say and how we say it. Words can cut like knives or be soothing to the soul. Pastor Jack W. Hayford says, "Just one word—whether ill-spoken or perfectly timed—can leave an imprint on a child's soul, an imprint that colors a lifetime of future behavior for better or for worse."[22] Maybe you can relate? I know I can. My mother often said, "Forgot is your middle name." That simple phrase stayed with me; it hurt because I genuinely would forget to do what I was told.

Proverbs 18:21 says, *"The tongue has the power of life and death, and those who love it will eat its fruit."* We all wish to be spoken to kindly. Kind words help to build trust and grow love within our children's hearts. In the Bible, James compares the tongue to a ship's rudder because small words coming out of our mouths can easily change our direction. (See James 3:4.) One word spoken in love can make a huge difference in a child's life. We are to guide, correct, and edify our children with our words.

---

22. Jack W. Hayford, *Blessing Your Children: Give the Gift that Will Change Their Lives Forever* (Bloomington, IN: Chosen Books, 2016), 45.

Tell your children often that you love them, you love being their parent, and you are so happy God chose you to be their parent. Spoken words, if heard often, can become a self-fulfilling prophecy. Instead of telling a child, "You are a troublemaker," ask, "Why are you causing trouble?" If children hear enough times that they are troublemakers, they will grow up believing that is who they are instead of believing who they are in Christ. If you have already used hurtful words or labels, ask for forgiveness and tell your child they are not whatever negative label you have placed upon them. Replace that memory with a positive one, using words that edify your child.

Truthfully, it hurts me to remember that I was sometimes harsh in my tone when I was angry. But I remember asking the Lord to help me soften my tone once I saw the look on my kids' faces. Praying for guidance gives us the power to change. Working on planting and nourishing a positive attitude within us will help our children learn how to become positive and less stressed as well. The moral code of children is developed by witnessing the conduct and the standards set by the adults in their lives.[23]

Dr. Kathy Koch lists many positive character traits that I believe are essential for parents, grandparents, caregivers, and ministry leaders to emulate in order to help their children become Christlike. Here are some of the traits she lists:

Bold, brave, caring, cheerful, compassionate, confident, consistent, courageous, dedicated, determined, devoted, discerning, faithful, forgiving, friendly, generous, gentle, grateful, honest, hopeful, humble, integrity, joyful, kind, loving, loyal, merciful, obedient, passionate, patient, peaceful persevering, polite, repentant, respectful, righteous, self-controlled, self-disciplined, servant, sincere,

---

23. Saul Mcleod, "Kohlberg's Stages of Moral Development," *Simply Psychology*, August 3, 2023, www.simplypsychology.org/kohlberg.html.

teachable, thankful, thoughtful, trustworthy, truthful, unselfish and wise.[24]

When you read these character traits, did one stand out? Maybe it's an attribute you already have, or perhaps it's a trait you would like to work on. In describing His character, Jesus says, *"I am gentle and humble in heart"* (Matthew 11:29). I love that!

Let our thoughts and words be guided by the Father, and let our actions do His work. Let our habits be in line with His will so that our character reflects His Holy Spirit that dwells within us. As best as we can, let our children witness heaven on earth in all we say and do with a humble heart.

INDECISIVE PARENTS

Many churches require couples to undergo premarital counseling before the pastor performs the wedding ceremony. But what is often overlooked in those sessions is the topic of child discipline. Just as each spouse is likely to have their own ideas about how relationships should work and use different communication techniques, they may not always agree on how to discipline children. One parent may believe the best way is to be stern and quick with doling out a consequence or correction when a child misbehaves, while the other prefers to lead with grace by giving more chances to "get it right" before a consequence is given.

If both parents are not united in their approach, disciplining their children can turn into an impossible task. It's crucial for mom and dad to agree on disciplinary methods.

I recall taking away a privilege for disobedience only to hear my son say, "Daddy said it's okay as long as I don't do it again." A

24. Dr. Kathy Koch, *Start with the Heart: How to Motivate Your Kids to Be Compassionate, Responsible, and Brave (Even When You're Not Around)* (Chicago, IL: Moody Publishers, 2019), 251–252.

child who is disciplined by one parent, goes to the other one, and manages to wiggle out of his consequence has manipulated both parents and will continue to do so. Indecisive parents or those who do not support each other's directives can cause irreversible problems that hinder children from becoming God-fearing, responsible adults.

In addition, God said, *"Let your 'Yes' be 'Yes,' and your 'No,' 'No'"* (Matthew 5:37 NKJV). This verse applies to all of us. Although you may say *maybe,* do so sparingly. *Maybe* can cause children to become anxious as they wait for a final decision.

NEGATIVE ACTIONS OF PARENTS

The last thing we want to do as Christian parents is to provoke or exasperate our children by:

+ Failing to keep our promises to them

+ Never admitting to being wrong

+ Purposely embarrassing them

+ Disciplining them harshly or unfairly

+ Demanding more than their abilities can handle

+ Picking favorites

+ Not listening to them

+ Being disrespectful toward them

+ Expressing negativity and indecisiveness

Any of these behaviors will cause our children to view Christianity as something to avoid or dislike.

It's frustrating for children to have parents who always say one thing but do another; they rarely *practice what they preach.* When a parent does not model what they are teaching about who God is and how He wants us to live, it will eventually put a strain on the parent/child relationship and ultimately on the child's belief system. How can a child trust a parent who claims to be a Christian but does not act in a way that supports that claim? Parents' words and actions hold much weight!

As I mentioned, my mother often said my middle name was *Forgot*. The name stuck with me my whole life as a negative thought from my mother. It's best not to label your child the *shy one*, the *loner*, the *chatterbox*, or anything along these lines. If repeated often enough, the child may believe it and live up to that label so that it becomes a self-fulfilling prophecy.

THE SILENT TREATMENT

When I was about five years old, I became mouthy and refused to listen to my mother; I was consistently disrespectful and disobedient. None of her discipline was working to change my behavior, and she finally reached her wit's end. Determined to win this battle of *who's in charge*, my mother decided not to speak to me until I understood and acknowledged what God meant when He commanded us to honor our parents. She did not answer my questions, she did not ask me questions, she did not speak to me…at all. She took care of me as always, dressing me, making dinner, and putting me to bed, but there was no conversation. At first, I dug in my heels, determined to stand my ground. But as that long day and night turned into a new morning, she still was not speaking to me, and I caved. I loved my mother and wanted more than anything to feel her love the way I always had. I apologized. We hugged, told each other how sorry we were, and promised to never use the silent treatment again.

Many children pout or give the silent treatment to someone with whom they're angry. Unfortunately, some parents have tried to correct this behavior by pouting or giving their child the silent treatment in return. Avoidance, apathy, or remaining detached is a form of psychological child abuse. This can cause great division and a broken bond between child and parent. When a child pouts or does not answer when spoken to, it is best to get down to their level and ask open-ended questions such as, "You seem sad (or angry); what happened?" To find out the motive for the undesired behavior, use a quiet voice and reassure the child that they are still loved. Some children may continue to be obstinate, but instead of demanding answers, tell them that you will be happy to talk with them when they are ready.

Ask heart-probing questions such as:

+ Why are you behaving this way?

+ Why are you angry?

+ Why will you not say, "I'm sorry"?

+ Why will you not accept the other person's apology?

+ What can you do differently so this doesn't happen again?

+ What other ways can you express your feelings without being angry or rude?

Most children will express their feelings when they feel they can safely do so, knowing that their parents will respect what they are saying and earnestly understand the reason behind their actions while seeking solutions.

5

CONTINUED CHARACTER DEVELOPMENT FOR OBEDIENT HEART TRANSFORMATION

Zachary grew up under the care of his grandmother, a single *mom* who worked tirelessly to care for and support him. Crystal worked in full-time ministry, which meant she didn't have a nine-to-five job; instead, she had to be available many evenings and every weekend. So Zachary spent a lot of time in the church's aftercare program, its evening programs for children, and childcare during the church's many special events. Church members, teachers, volunteers, and staff made an active investment in Zachary, modeling God's love to him. He was poured into by the people there so much that he has become a faithful young adult volunteer in the church that he attends. That investment of time, love, and care enriched the soil that I have talked about, ultimately transforming Zachary's heart by the power of the Holy Spirit.

I love to hear or read how God's Word transforms hearts. We all need transformation—some more than others. Oh, did I just say that? Yes, sorry, but it's the truth! And God's angels rejoice when an unsaved, abusive father or mother transforms into a man or woman of faith.

This happened in a true story that was expressed in song and made into one of my all-time favorite movies, *I Can Only Imagine*.[25] Bart, a self-disciplined and focus-driven man, became a disciple for Christ despite the suffering and pain of his childhood.

The transformation Christ brings is necessary to become a saved sinner. This transformation can come from the discipline of conversion.

HONOR AND RESPECT

When my son was five, he was a Junior Olympic Taekwondo champion. He was extremely happy that his hard work and perseverance allowed him to achieve this recognition. Taekwondo taught martial arts, but more importantly, it taught my son self-control, restraint, respect, confidence, and honor. Learning the concept of honor is best understood through honorable interactions among family members, which makes for a peaceful home environment.

There's a difference between respect and honor. Respect displays an attitude of high regard and is demonstrated by having good manners, being polite, and showing care for others. Honor expresses thoughtfulness. Children honor their parents when they do a task without being asked, such as making their beds without being reminded, or voluntarily helping with housework.

On the flip side, dishonor and disrespectfulness should be dealt with swiftly. If you don't nip disrespect in the bud, it will grow into an uncontrollable weed, resulting in negative behavior and damaging consequences. Respecting authority is critical to a child's ability to understand what it means to respect God and His commandments.

Martin Luther wisely claims, "In short, there is no greater or nobler authority on earth than that of parents over their children,

---

25. *I Can Only Imagine*, directed by Andrew and Jon Erwin (2018; Lionsgate/Roadside Attractions).

for this authority is both spiritual and temporal."[26] Likewise, he and his followers believed that "a systematic program of religious and *ethical indoctrination* would have results...the products of disciplined, hard human work."[27] (The emphasis is mine.) Such a program also makes for respectful and honorable children—at least we hope so!

I don't know about you, but it is a pet peeve of mine when someone does not say *please* or *thank you*. I have to bite my tongue when I hold the door open for someone, and they walk right past me without a word, as if I were their private doorman. These days, we not only witness a lack of respect, but we see increasing instances of disrespect as well.

The son of a friend of mine is one of the most respectful employees at his company. He's kind to others, opens doors for all, doesn't talk over anyone else, shows up on time, and goes above and beyond to complete a task without being asked. When someone asked him where he learned to be that kind of guy, he shrugged and replied, "It's just how my parents raised me to show respect." What a compliment to this young man's parents! When we teach our children the importance of being respectful, we set them up to be successful in relationships. Respect for other people and for God is an important virtue, and good manners often stem from respect.

ENCOURAGEMENT OVER REWARDS

We all love to hear encouraging words, which motivate us to do good. This motivation comes from within our hearts and helps to combat any lack of resiliency that can weaken it.

26. Jane E. Strohl, "The Child in Luther's Theology: 'For What Purpose Do We Older Folks Exist, Other Than to Care for...the Young?'" in *The Child in Christian Thought*, ed. Marcia J. Bunge (Grand Rapids, MI: Wm. B. Eerdmans Publishing Co., 2001), 140.
27. Ibid., 144.

There are two types of motivation: intrinsic, which comes from within, making people want to do good for others; and extrinsic, which comes from doing good in order to receive a reward.

Children brought up in the same home with the same parents rarely behave the same way. Even identical twins have their own personalities and ways of processing the world. One child may have more intrinsic motivation, making her bed daily, putting her clothes away, and willingly helping her mom with chores. She is motivated to do these things simply because she knows it makes her mother happy—and that makes her happy. Her sister may have more extrinsic motivation, wondering, "What will I get if I do that?" If she takes it upon herself to do extra chores, she will run to Mom or Dad and ask for additional dollars in her allowance or a special privilege. The extrinsically motivated child wants to know a reward is coming for good behavior before deciding it is worth the effort.

We hope our children's hearts will desire to do what is right without constantly being told to do so for selfish gain.

STRONG-WILLED CHILDREN

Rachel is the natural wild child in her family. Unlike her brother and her parents, she's strong-willed and hard to tame. Her often exasperated mother says, "Rachel is God's way of teaching me how to be more patient!" For her quiet and reserved mother, Rachel's spirit is hard to understand or parent.

Children can be disruptive, fierce, uncontrollable, or simply sinful. Until *they* learn self-control, *we* will have to be their self-control. At an early age, they need to master not only the difference between right and wrong but also acceptable behavior versus unacceptable behavior. It gets harder as they get older because when they are young, we know their every move.

Hopefully, children will learn to want to do what is right because their motivation will come from their hearts to please their parents and the Lord.

Whatever you do, work at it will all your heart, as working for the Lord, not for human masters, since you know that you will receive an inheritance from the Lord as a reward. It is the Lord Christ you are serving. (Colossians 3:23–24)

In addition, before we address a situation, it's good to note that there is a difference between childish behavior and foolishness. We know that children naturally act with immature tendencies. However, they can become foolish when we give them clear instructions that they understand and yet *choose not to follow those instructions.*

Intentional Parents International founders Phil and Diane Comer ask:

What about those times when you just don't know if something your child is doing even warrants discipline? This can lead to confusion and inconsistency, which is why we came up with the Ten-Year Rule. Just ask yourself, *What will this behavior or attitude look like in ten years?*[28]

God's Word states, *"Blessed is the one you discipline,* Lord, *the one you teach from your law; you grant them relief from days of trouble"* (Psalm 94:12–13). Paul writes, *"Fathers, do not exasperate your children; instead, bring them up in the training and instruction **of the Lord"** (Ephesians 6:4). Notice that this training and instruction is not *of the law* because Jesus is the perfect way and the perfect law.

---

28. Phil and Diane Comer, *Raising Passionate Jesus Followers: The Power of Intentional Parenting* (Grand Rapids, MI: Zondervan, 2018), 71.

It is a relationship with the Lord Jesus Christ and the love of Him that change hearts, not pharisaical laws that tell us to obey.

ENTITLEMENT IS A COMMON PROBLEM

Children love to receive gifts, money—you name it! Well, don't we all? My friend's daughter was highly disappointed that she didn't get the designer purse she wanted for her birthday. Her mother explained that money was tight since Dad was laid off from his job. The daughter replied, "But I want it! Don't you have money in the bank you can get?" Her mother had unknowingly encouraged her daughter's selfish, entitled attitude by always buying her the expensive gifts that she wanted. My friend was deeply hurt by her daughter's mindset.

An attitude of entitlement can cause major problems later in life when people don't give in to our children's demands. A child having a temper tantrum isn't pretty, but an adult sulking or raging is even worse.

Rather than giving children an allowance, let them earn money by doing age-appropriate chores. They will place more value on anything they purchase with money they've earned for a job well done, giving them a sense of pride and accomplishment. Children will soon develop an attitude of gratitude. Also, they should only be *paid* for chores established ahead of time while also having unpaid chores that contribute to the family. This will teach them that being a part of a family includes responsibilities, and Mom and Dad will enjoy having a helping hand around the home.

BLAMING AND TATTLING

I'm sure you've experienced something like this: "Mom, I didn't break the toy; *he* broke it!" Followed by, "No, Mom, *she* did it!" Or perhaps your teenage daughter has run into the kitchen, yelling that her little sister won't stay out of her room. Listening to our children pass the blame and tattle on each other can be irritating!

I remember a time when my three-year-old daughter and my five-year-old son were playing in our driveway. My daughter fell and yelled, "Guy! Why you do dat?" The look on his face was priceless—because he was nowhere near her! I lovingly kissed her booboo and told her that blaming her brother for something he didn't do was a lie, and lying is a sin.

Tattling is one reason Joseph got in trouble with his brothers. (See Genesis 37:2–7.) Some children like to tattle because they want to solve the issue or let you know that *they* know right from wrong. Some like to tattle to try to get other children in trouble.

While tattling can be wrong, informing an adult that someone is in danger of getting hurt, either emotionally or physically, is always acceptable. "Mommy, Johnny is playing with a knife" is sharing information, not tattling. That child should receive a positive acknowledgment that Jesus sees and hears everything, and He is happy that she did the right thing for Johnny. Author and parenting coach Lori Wildenberg once suggested that I define tattling and telling this way: "Tattling gets someone into trouble. Telling gets someone out of trouble."

Scripture tells us we're supposed to go to our brother with problems and talk to him. (See Matthew 18:15.) When your child tattles on their sibling or another family member, sit down with them and explain that they need to learn to work things out before they come to you. Make sure they understand that you will not always be their referee. If they cannot work out these simple disputes lovingly, they will not be able to play together or will lose a privilege.

I have heard many stories from parents who have creatively handled conflicts among their kids. When used correctly, solutions like *leader of the day* give a child the opportunity to learn how to make decisions, resolve conflicts, and act responsibly. One unique way I discovered was having two little kids wear one XXL adult-sized T-shirt, with their unhappy little faces side by side, their heads together. They were told they could not take the shirt off until they worked out their problem!

Children practice learning to use a fork, ride a bike, brush their teeth, and many other things. They also need to practice learning right behavior and conflict resolution. Once our children understand that we will not engage in something they can work out on their own, they will be less likely to tattle, which can produce a more peaceful and loving atmosphere in the home and elsewhere.

Also, we need to tell our children that blaming others or making excuses for what they themselves wrongfully did is a form of pride, and it hurts God's heart. Proverbs 28:13 states, *"Whoever conceals their sins does not prosper, but the one who confesses and renounces them finds mercy."* Confessing and repenting sin can be hard, but we need to motivate our children to do both. No one likes an adult who never takes responsibility for their wrongdoings. It can cause serious problems later in life in their work, marriage, or relationships. We are helping our children to practice the right thoughts, the right words to speak, and the right behavior to exhibit.

TEASING AND BULLYING

Maybe you have experienced being teased or bullied at some point in your childhood. It's a common problem. Bragging, teasing, or bullying are never acceptable and should be dealt with swiftly. Often, when children feel insecure or have been bullied, they inflict hurtful behavior on other children. But such actions can also be caused by exhaustion, illness, hunger, frustration, jealousy, anxiety, or a lack of self-control. It's best to find out the reason for the behavior before reacting or admonishing.

Loving a bully can be a hard concept for children to understand. It depends upon each child's cognitive ability and social makeup. However, we are called to teach our children to love their enemies and leave it up to God to transform their hearts.

Ginger Hubbard, an author and speaker who homeschooled her children, addresses many issues such as tattling, whining, lying, teasing, and bragging. She says:

> We have approximately eighteen wonderful years to train our children in righteousness. If only we could view all their verbal offenses as precious opportunities to teach them, surely then we would respond righteously whenever these offenses present themselves. We wouldn't feel inconvenienced, angered, or frustrated when our children blow it. Instead, we would be thankful, joyful, and eager for the chance to point them to Christ and his power to transform lives.[29]

Help your child understand that sometimes, no matter how nice, kind, and loving they are toward a child who is mean and nasty, their kindness may not change the other's behavior. This affords a great lesson learned early: we may not be able to control others, but we can learn to control how others' actions affect us. Children and adults alike should not let someone's anger destroy the love they have.

FORGIVE THE BULLY

A few kids were mean to me in elementary school. They would call me ugly names, make fun of my clothes, and tease me into tears. I was raised by a single mother, and we couldn't afford the newest toys or clothes. If I had learned how to forgive their

---

29. Ginger Hubbard, *I Can't Believe You Just Said That! Biblical Wisdom for Taming Your Child's Tongue* (Nashville, TN: Nelson Books, 2018), 5.

actions, my actions toward them would have been different and could have diffused the situation. When children learn early that when they love and forgive others, the aggressors lose the power to hurt them—and they learn that their offenders need their love and the love of Jesus. Also, the bully is more likely to stop his hurtful words and actions when he no longer receives a negative reaction.

Children can learn early that love covers a multitude of sins. Proverbs 25:21–22 tells us, *"If your enemy is hungry, give him food to eat; if he is thirsty, give him water to drink. In doing this, you will heap burning coals on his head, and the LORD will reward you."* By demonstrating love to those who hate us, we can help to purify their hearts and minds. Hot coals and the Word of God are purifying. Jesus loved His enemies and prayed for them.

Teaching children to pray for their bullies, and not stepping in as a parent to rescue them from every offense, is a beneficial biblical concept. Pastor and counselor Reb Bradley suggests:

> Do not rescue your children from every playmate who offends them by scolding the offender or intervening to make everything fair. Instead, help them view their offenders through the eyes of love. A child continually rescued from offensive people grows to see themselves as victims deserving of pity or special protection.[30]

A poor-me attitude can cripple a child from becoming an adult who actively seeks to do their best in all areas of life.

SAYING "I'M SORRY" AND ASKING FOR FORGIVENESS

I remember reading about a woman who didn't talk to her daughter for twenty-five years. I can't even imagine or wrap my

---

30. Bradley, *Child Training Tips*, 127.

mind around that. That is a lifetime of not speaking to your child! It breaks my heart to think about their lost years. Family estrangement is not only painful, it's unbiblical. God calls us as the body of Christ to love, support, and forgive.

When someone harms me through their words or actions, and they never apologize, I admit it does anger me. The words "I'm sorry" benefit the one who was wronged as well as the one who said or did something hurtful. A genuine apology needs to be conveyed not only in words but also in actions.

Children need to apologize, discuss what they did wrong, and what they can do to avoid that situation again. They also need to accept responsibility instead of blaming others in their apology.

Mankind's failure to accept responsibility began in the garden of Eden, when Adam and Eve ate of the Tree of Knowledge of Good and Evil. (See Genesis 3.) Adam quickly blamed Eve, who blamed the serpent, who had no one to blame but his own lying, sinful nature. Regardless of who sinned first, it didn't keep God from withholding punishment for any of them.

Children should also make restitution if damage is done. If they broke someone's toy on purpose, then the toy needs to be replaced, perhaps with one of their own. Help your child understand that they should ask for forgiveness from the person and from God as well. Likewise, encourage them to pray that whomever they offended would forgive them.

On the flip side, children who learn how to forgive without harboring a retributive desire can help other children who need to receive unconditional love. Jesus gives us the perfect example of such love, forgiving His enemies even as He was dying on the cross! (See Luke 23:34.) Help your children understand that bullies may act the way they do because they may be hurting for reasons we don't know or understand. The adage, "Hurt people hurt people" rings true.

If children realize that Jesus is watching and their parents will likely find out what happened, they might be motivated to choose good behavior. Also, tell your child, "You may be doing something behind someone's back, but you're doing it in front of God's eyes."

PROPER BEHAVIOR CAN BE LEARNED EARLY

Some parents say, "I don't like to be too hard on my kids because they are only little for such a short time, and I want them to have fun while they are young." Let's acknowledge that our children have only one childhood and, yes, we want them to enjoy it. But we also want our children to make wise choices that lead to obedience and responsibility. If we wait and put *fun* over good behavior, we might wind up with a twenty-two-year-old who still acts like a five-year-old—but their bad behavior won't be limited to a broken toy or refusal to go to bed on time. It could be drunk driving or stealing something. And your adult child will look to you to bail them out time and time again.

In addition, when we allow our children to quit a sport because they cry when it is too hard or stop participating in an activity they committed to because it's no longer fun, we are encouraging a defeatist attitude. In essence, we're telling them it's okay to walk away from anything that is demanding or uninteresting, that they cannot work through their feelings or the circumstances they are facing. There may be legitimate exceptions. But if a child is not taught how to persevere, how will they become resilient adults?

Children will try to avoid taking responsibility for their actions by:

+ Minimizing them, saying things like, "It's not that bad; nobody got hurt."

+ Rationalizing them, such as emulating something they saw on a TV show.

+ Denying them, saying, "I didn't do it!"

+ Avoiding authority by running away from Mommy.

+ Sharing their guilt, saying, "Everyone else is doing it!"

+ Using emotional manipulation, such as batting their big, sweet eyes.

Oh, but those big eyes are hard to resist as they plead their case of innocence!

6

BUILDING A STRONG CHRISTIAN FOUNDATION

Once we have grasped some great ideas to help disciple our children, we can move toward building a strong foundation in Christ or repairing any cracks that we find.

Ask most kids where they go to find answers to their questions in life, and they will say Google, websites, social media, chat rooms, or their friends. Scary, right?

G. K. Chesterton (1874–1936), considered to be one of the best writers of the twentieth century, once said, "Without education, we are in a horrible and deadly danger of taking educated people seriously."

Wait! What did he say? Pause and read it again. I had to read it twice. It makes sense when we consider that:

> *Attaining to the whole measure of the fullness of Christ...we will no longer be infants, tossed back and forth by the waves, and blown here and there by every wind of teaching and by the cunning and craftiness of people in their deceitful scheming.*
> (Ephesians 4:13–14)

There are many people who claim to be experts on specific subjects—or act as if they are. Some experts can be *expertly* wrong, hence Chesterton's warning. In this chapter, we'll examine how we can gain and instill biblical wisdom early in our children while remembering that it is also never too late. God's Word is truth, and key concepts, built upon introductory truths, help *prepare the soil* to become fertile ground in which to *plant the seeds of biblical wisdom* later. The Word of God holds the answers to our parenting questions, and God is the expert!

INSTILLING BIBLICAL WISDOM

A foundation of Christian doctrine that is not deeply rooted in our children's hearts could allow false religion to one day penetrate through the proverbial cracks and crevices. Or perhaps our children's faith will be unstable, like seeds that were planted on rocky soil, which represents those *"who receive the word with joy… but they have no root"* (Luke 8:13). The truth is that our children *will* be indoctrinated either by a secular worldview or a biblical one.

Teaching our children using principles, guidelines, and rules based in truth will introduce and instill Christian values in them. Because we love our children and want their hearts and minds to learn the truth, we use God's Word to teach them Christian doctrine, which is:

> The body of teachings of the Christian faith concerning its central beliefs. Doctrine is grounded in Scripture and aims to maintain the integrity of Christianity by distinguishing it from non-Christian beliefs. Doctrine is of central importance in Christian preaching and teaching in that it equips the people of God for effective and faithful service in his world.[31]

---

31. Martin H. Manser, et al., *Dictionary of Bible Themes: The Accessible and Comprehensive Tool for Topical Studies* (London: Logos Bible Software, 2009).

It is important to understand the difference between brainwashing and indoctrination. Brainwashing is psychological manipulation and coercion. Biblical indoctrination is helping someone accept God's Word as truth so that they reject anything that contradicts His Word.

BUILDING A SOLID FOUNDATION

When I was around eight years old, I was invited to attend my friend's Sunday school class. In a loving manner and fun environment, that Sunday school teacher instilled biblical doctrine and principles. She taught us about Jesus's characteristics and His sacrifice. In my young heart, she also planted the seeds of *how* to think, not just *what* to think. I looked forward to going every Sunday.

Parents are usually the ones who teach their children about the spiritual aspects of life, yet parents may struggle in this area. Perhaps they weren't taught by their own parents.

Some parents might rely on a Sunday school teacher, pastor, or ministry leader to teach their children how to follow Christ. However, when we give up the responsibility to spiritually develop our children—for whatever reason—they may begin to think that faith is irrelevant. It's alarming how many ministry leaders today do not speak, model, or even follow biblical doctrine. Christian apologist Ken Ham states, "In an age of pluralism, atheism, and skepticism, a 'Sunday school' faith built on stories alone won't cut it out there in the real world. Instead, our children's faith will be easily and quickly devoured by worldly philosophy, demonic deception, and unbelief."[32]

George Barna believes that parents need to start spiritual training when children are very young because "waiting too long

32. Ken Ham, *Ready to Return? The Need for a Fundamental Shift in Church Culture to Save a Generation* (Green Forest, AR: New Leaf Publishing Group, 2015), 96.

produces unfortunate outcomes for parents and children."[33] It may take years and much suffering before one believes in Christ if not taught early in life. Again, it's never too late! God can do amazing things at any age and at any stage of life. But starting early should make those teenage years less stressful as you build a solid cornerstone of faith.

A child rooted in the good news will learn to obey God's commandments and understand that His law is a blessing to them. Blessed is the child *"whose delight is in the law of the* LORD, *and who meditates on his law day and night"* (Psalm 1:2).

GIFTS, TALENTS, AND GOD'S PLAN

It's helpful to discover our children's gifts or talents as soon as possible. As a kid, I liked to wiggle my ears. My friends thought this was cool. I wish I had a better talent to tell you about, but unfortunately, that was it.

Gregory's talent as a little boy was much more impressive. He was raised by a single mom who worked long hours as a court reporter. His grandmother was his after-school babysitter from the time he was in preschool. She loved to cook—sometimes from a recipe and at other times from an idea that popped into her head. Gregory loved to hold her cookbook and read the words he knew to help Grandma. More often than not, he would excitedly suggest how they should change the recipe to create something new that they would taste and critique later. Her love of creative cooking and her heart for nurturing her grandson created a passion in Gregory, who grew up to become the head chef at a restaurant known for its unique entrées.

Perhaps you have a budding artist, singer, athlete, or engineer in your family. Many times, children take after a talented relative.

33. George Barna, *Transforming Children into Spiritual Champions* (Ventura, CA: Regal Books, 2003), 82.

As children grow spiritually, you may see the gifts given by the Holy Spirit.

How wonderful it is when someone we love offers guidance, encouragement, and prayers for us to succeed. We feel loved and valued. We should also encourage, guide, pray, and equip our children to use their talents, gifts, and dreams to serve others. The sooner we recognize their unique abilities and desires, the more time we will have to help them sharpen their skills to be used to glorify God.

As you pray for your children, offer opportunities to showcase their talents and gifts. While encouraging them along the way, God will reveal His plan and purpose for them. Something that may seem silly now may prove to be beneficial later. Remember, David was a youth with a slingshot! (See 1 Samuel 17:40.) *"Do not despise these small beginnings, for the LORD rejoices to see the work begin"* (Zechariah 4:10 NLT).

ESTABLISH ROUTINES EARLY

Many adults have a routine or schedule to get them through the day. I like to have a cup of coffee and read my Bible before I begin work. Routines are also important for children and can be a way to instill biblical principles consistently. Predictability also brings security and stability to a child's life.

Every morning, my children would say a prayer before they got out of bed—just a simple prayer such as, "Good morning, Jesus, I love You." After they brushed their teeth and got dressed, I would say, "Jesus, Mommy, and Daddy love that you prayed and brushed your teeth. Now you are ready for the day!"

Before you drop your preschooler off at school, hug your child and say, "Jesus will be with you today because He's in your heart, and Mommy will pick you up soon." When your child goes to play at a friend's house, say something like, "Jesus and I know you will be nice and kind." As I wrote in the introduction, many of these suggestions can be tweaked to apply to older children, such as, "Don't forget to pray before you take your final exam," or, "Remember God is watching all you do—make Him proud."

Deuteronomy 6:7 is a mandate to teach and instruct our children when we are at home, when we walk together along the road, when lie down before we sleep, and when we start our day—meaning all the time! Seminary professor Howard Hendricks notes, "Spiritual growth should not be compartmentalized but integrated with every other aspect of life...intellectually, physically, socially, and emotionally."[34]

ATTENDING CHURCH SHOULD BE SECOND NATURE

Sunday morning is the most challenging day of Maxine's week. She and her husband Ray have always been active members of a local church. They both volunteer; she helps in the children's ministry, and he works in the bookstore. Ray's career is in the publishing industry, so his expertise makes him the perfect person to oversee the entire store operation. Every Sunday, Ray leaves home at 6:00 a.m., leaving Maxine alone to get their three children out of bed, fed, dressed, into the car, and off to church. Some weeks, Maxine struggles through Sunday mornings to the point of wanting to throw in the towel and just stay home. But she doesn't do that because church is a priority in their family. Instead, Maxine prays for patience and peace as she gets her children prepared to attend church and worship God.

Church is where we meet, learn, and pray for one another, and there are only a few legitimate reasons for not going. Maybe the car won't start, a child has a fever, or the dog ate the car keys. (Dogs have been known to eat crazy things.) Aside from sickness

---

34. Hendricks, *Teaching to Change Lives*, 25.

or something we can't do anything about, church should be a priority. The Word of God instructs:

> *Let us consider how we may spur one another on toward love and good deeds, not giving up meeting together, as some are in the habit of doing, but encouraging one another—and all the more as you see the Day approaching.* (Hebrews 10:24–25)

Some people claim it is not right to *force* their children to go to church. However, if children find out that being *forced* is a way to get out of doing something they don't want to do, guess who is running the household? God tells us that children must *"honor your father and your mother, so that you may live long in the land the* Lord *your God is giving you"* (Exodus 20:12). Teaching our children the importance of obedience and making them do righteous things like going to church, despite their opinion, will help them become godly adults. Sometimes we must do things we don't want to do, but we need to do what is right.

Exodus 34:14 says, *"Do not worship any other god, for the* Lord, *whose name is Jealous, is a jealous God."* God is not jealous like we might be; He is jealous *for* man, not willing to share His creation with a foreign god. God wants us to worship Him by singing songs, praying, and hearing His Word. Worship is evidence of a pure heart and total devotion to the Lord.

Encouraging children to sing by offering many opportunities to break out in song is faith in action. Most kids love to sing their favorite tunes. You can hear them hum a familiar melody or belt out a favorite song from school or church. They have an amazing ability to remember words and music that touch their hearts. Teach them to put their memory verses from Sunday school into a song they can sing. Have them make up *worship words* to a tune they already know. Encourage your little ones to sing a thank-you to God for something they are grateful for. Not only are you spending quality moments with your little ones, but you are pointing them toward the habit of worshipping and singing to the Lord.

MAKING MOMENTS MATTER

Take every opportunity and use every tool available to instill biblical doctrines regarding God, Jesus, the Holy Spirit, His Word, sin, salvation, and the love of Christ. Share the creation story from Genesis 1. Add another moment by telling your children about Noah's ark, a great story about sin, salvation, creation, and redemption in Genesis 6–9. Look for opportunities to talk to your teenagers. Just remember to listen more, talk less, and then let them determine when the conversation is over. That way, they will feel safe talking another time.

After reading biblical stories, ask your children to retell them in their own words. It can be very amusing to hear their version. For example, did you know King Saul had many wives and porcupines? It's also fun to let your child teach what they have learned back to the family and let older children lead the family devotional time. The learning pyramid diagram developed by the National Training Laboratory shows that after a twenty-four-hour period, students retain 90 percent of what they learn when they teach others.[35]

Sacred play is another way to discover Jesus. When children's spiritual playtimes are lovingly guided and not encumbered with rules and regulations, they have a greater chance of developing a deeper faith that solidifies the biblical principles we want to instill in our children.

Other children and siblings have great influence, and your child should play with children who are being taught the same godly truth you wish to instill within your child. After all, their siblings and friends will most likely be in their lives after you are gone.

---

35. "The Learning Pyramid," *Education Corner: Education That Matters*, www. educationcorner.com/the-learning-pyramid.html.

PLAYTIME IS LEARNING TIME

As a child, what was your favorite time of the day? I bet many would say playtime. As adults, we still love to have our playtime. My playtime is when I get to sit down and read a book or take a walk outside. Reading educational books and walking through nature feed my mind and my soul. Albert Einstein once said, "Play is the highest form of research." Playtime enriches children's social, physical, emotional, and cognitive development and is a tool to help them understand their fears, desires, needs, wants, and much more. The best playtime is when your child can play with you. I used to let my daughter put makeup on my face, and we would laugh at the results. That one-on-one time affords a special connection and bond with the parent.

Use one-on-one time to incorporate truth and learning into play with your kids. Whether it is building blocks, reading books, coloring, or playing outside, use that time to ask your children questions that may point to opportunities to learn more about God, such as, "What's one thing you'd like to learn about God?" or "What do you love about Jesus?" Then take note of their answers and look for books, resources, or games that may help them discover their own answers. Kids appreciate knowing that they were right in their assessments, and they learn and retain more when they are having fun. Let's help our children have fun while transforming their hearts and minds for Christ! In the last chapter, I share ideas on how to make learning time fun and purposeful.

ENCOUNTERING JESUS BRINGS TRANSFORMATION

I remember having two encounters with Jesus as a young child. The first was when my mother was sick, and I was afraid she would die. I prayed every night and every day that Jesus would keep her alive. One day, I felt the peace of the Holy Spirit and knew that my mother would be okay. The second encounter was when I lived next door to a bully who would often hit me during the walk home from school. One day, she started walking toward me, and I began to back away from her. Suddenly, I felt I should stop and look behind me—I was about to fall into a deep ravine! I ran as fast as I could past her, and when I got home, I thanked Jesus. I knew it was His Holy Spirit that made me glance back. I would have been seriously injured if I hadn't done so. These incidents drew me closer to Christ and transformed my heart.

When children experience personal encounters with Jesus, they receive both intellectual and empirical knowledge that will connect their hearts to the Savior. When your child makes a decision to give their life to Jesus, celebrate that fantastic step in faith! Give them a lasting memento to mark the occasion. Help them understand what it means to be a *new creation* because of their decision.

The metamorphosis of a caterpillar into a butterfly helps us understand our own conversion from sinner to believer. The butterfly's transformation is physical, but ours is spiritual and the most amazing and important change we can make. Paul personally witnessed his own incredible metamorphosis! (See Acts 9.)

DON'T FORGET THE HOLY SPIRIT

As a child, I thought the Holy Spirit was an angel. Figuring out who He was and understanding what He did was difficult for me. The earlier children learn about the Holy Spirit, the quicker they will love Him like they love God the Father, Jesus, Mom, and Dad.

Author and television host Pamela Christian says:

The Holy Spirit's role in Jesus' human life is often unappreciated. The Spirit brought about the incarnation (Luke 1:35), anointed Jesus for his earthly ministry at His baptism, (Matthew 3:16; Mark 1:10; Luke 3:21–22), filled Jesus with the Holy Spirit (Luke 4:1), led and empowered Jesus (Luke 4:14, 18) and raised Jesus from the dead (Romans 8:11).[36]

Evangelist Anne Graham Lotz explains the wonderful works of the Holy Spirit:

The very promise Jesus gave us contains a name for the Holy Spirit that reveals the uniqueness of His nearness in our loneliness. This name, "Comforter," is equally translated from the Greek text into six other names, each of which describes a slightly different aspect of the Holy Spirit's precious, personal ministry in our lives:

Comforter: One Who relieves of mental distress.

Counselor: One Who gives advice and manages causes.

Helper: One Who furnishes relief or support.

Intercessor: One Who acts between parties to reconcile differences.

Advocate: One Who pleads the cause of another.

Strengthener: One Who causes strength and endurance.

Standby: One Who can be always relied upon.[37]

The Holy Spirit wants us and our children to have a relationship with Him. He wants to give us strength and guidance so that we can help ourselves and others. It's important to speak about the Holy Spirit and what He does for your child. The Holy Spirit

---

36. Pamela Christian, *Revive Your Life! Rest for Your Anxious Heart* (Yorba Linda, CA: Protocol, Ltd., 2017), 106.

37. Anne Graham Lotz, "The Wonderful Someone," *Hugh's News*, February 14, 2019, www.hughsnews.com/newsletter-posts/the-wonderful-someone-by-anne-graham-lotz.

is the one who transforms us to become like Christ. Help your children to pray daily to the Holy Spirit just like they pray to God or Jesus.

LET'S DISCUSS EDUCATION

Children learn best in environments suited to their personalities and mindsets. Some do well in a private school with more structure; others do better in homeschool, where they are not constrained by strict schedules or group expectations. Perhaps a hybrid homeschool/classroom program is the best fit for some children.

It is important to pray over your decisions about each child's educational path, asking God to guide you toward the right schools and programs for their unique needs.

I wholeheartedly believe in homeschooling, if possible, but some parents cannot do this, nor can they afford to send their children to a private Christian school. Statistics show that 88 percent of children in America are in the public school system.

Unfortunately, public schools today are vastly different than they were just ten years ago. They have increasingly become a training field for secular humanism, which tries to instill anti-Christian values and doctrines, teach socialistic ideology, and corrupt the minds and souls of the next generation. The Freedom from Religion Foundation actively supports the restriction of any religion in public schools, therefore helping to bar prayer or religious instruction. Evolution is taught rather than creationism because the latter is considered to be religious teaching. But as Ken Ham points out, "Secular groups contradict themselves by teaching their own brand of religion (naturalism — atheism) in the public schools. And the government uses our tax dollars to do it."[38]

---

38. Ham, *Ready to Return*, 59.

Some Christian parents believe our children should be placed in public schools to serve as the salt and light there. But children must be trained for spiritual battle before being sent to war. If unprepared, they may lose their saltiness—their ability to defend what they believe. Jesus says, "*You are the salt of the earth. But if the salt loses its saltiness, how can it be made salty again?*" (Matthew 5:13).

Ham notes:

> Children are being contaminated as a result of their secular education, television, the books they read, [social media] and their friends. In a world of no absolutes, evolution, sex outside marriage, gay "marriage," attacks on gender distinction...How do they know which way to go?[39]

Adolf Hitler once said, "He alone, who owns the youth, gains the future,"[40] and the devil knows this as well. Children must first be uncontaminated and filled with God's Word and faith before we send them out into the world.

We need to show them truth through absolutes, and God's nature is the best classroom. Nature is an absolute; it is never subjective. The sun rises in the east and sets in the west. Rain falls from the sky. Trees and plants grow from the ground. God's creation is the baseline to teach about absolutes, leading them away from the false narratives that Satan wishes to impose. I recommend Eryn Lynum's book *Rooted in Wonder*,[41] which connects the Word of God and His creation to teach children about absolutes and the truth.

---

39. Ibid., 163.
40. Ibid., 70.
41. Eryn Lynum, *Rooted in Wonder: Nurturing Your Family's Faith Through God's Creation* (Grand Rapids, MI: Kregel Publications, 2023).

Homeschooling is the best choice for your children because they belong to you, not the state. There are many wonderful organizations available to help you, such as the Homeschool Legal Defense Association,[42] which advocates for the right to homeschool. Support HSLDA if you can do so. Also, watch the documentary *Schoolhouse Rocked: The Homeschool Revolution* by Yvette and Garritt Hampton; it details what is happening in the public school system and how we are on the verge of losing the right to choose how to educate our children.[43] In addition, Kirk Cameron's *The Homeschool Awakening* helps families on a mission to place faith and fun into the learning journey.[44] The education they receive will shape their worldview and help formulate the adults they will become.

I remember the first day I took my children to their Christian preschool. I was more worried than they were. Thank the Lord they were happy to go, so excited to play with other children and know they were *going to a big school* like their cousins. I was happy for them but my momma heart was sad. I wasn't ready to let them go, but I felt comforted knowing I'd chosen the right place for them.

Preschoolers love action. They want to sing, dance, play with puppets, make things with their hands, and create and recreate games. Between the ages of three and five, they can grasp the idea that Jesus did wondrous things, such as walking on the water, healing sick people, and calming the scary storm.

An excellent teaching tool is to invite children to wonder or reflect by issuing *wonder statements* such as, "I wonder what Jesus looks like in heaven."[45] Play a game, "What would Jesus do or what

---

42. Learn more at hslda.org.
43. schoolhouserocked.com.
44. www.thehomeschoolawakening.com.
45. Scottie May, "The Contemplative-Reflective Model," in *Perspectives on Children's Spiritual Formation: 4 Views*, ed. Michael J. Anthony (Nashville, TN: Broadman & Holman Publishers, 2006), 71.

can God do if...? Or when in the outdoor classroom, ask, "Why do you think God made the clouds?" The goal of the game is to encourage kids to wonder and explore in their faith.

When choosing a preschool, pick one that reflects the love of Jesus and offers visual, auditory, kinesthetic, social, and solitary opportunities for learning. Every child has a different learning style and way of perceiving and retaining information. In her book, *8 Great Smarts*, Dr. Kathy Koch describes the best ways children naturally think and retain information. Some children are word smart, meaning they learn best through reading and talking. Other children are picture smart and learn better by visually seeing what is being taught. Still others are music smart, retaining what they learn more readily by adding a music element. Other children are logic smart, body smart, nature smart, or self-smart, while many are a combination of these.[46]

It's beneficial to research any school, summer camp, or program your children may be attending and have a list of questions ready. Make sure the organization's childcare philosophy and mission match your own. Find out the ratio of workers to children, not including maintenance or kitchen staff. How do they discipline children? Are parents encouraged to drop in anytime to check on their little ones? What age-specific programs do they offer?

A CORD OF THREE STRANDS

Family, church, and school need to work together. *"A cord of three strands is not quickly broken"* (Ecclesiastes 4:12). Children who are given the opportunity to apply what they learn to authentic situations are prepared to figure out complex solutions to problems when they attend higher academia.

---

46. Dr. Kathy Koch, *8 Great Smarts: Discover and Nurture Your Child's Intelligences* (Chicago, IL: Moody Publishers, 2016).

We are engaged in spiritual warfare, and we must use our strongest, sharpest, and most precise weapon to bring godly morality back into public education: Prayer.

Pray against the influence of secular culture, which uses lies and deception as a method of reasoning. Pray for laws to be enacted to protect children who attend public school from all that is anti-Christian. Pray that families will never be stripped of their rights to a homeschool education.

It is amazing to learn that we are spiritually hardwired to be connected to God through prayer. In Dr. Lisa Miller's book, *The Awakened Brain*, she summarizes notable findings by Dr. Kenneth Kendler and his colleagues at Virginia Commonwealth University:

> He found that there is significant genetic contribution to spirituality. Specifically, our capacity for a personal spiritual life is *29 percent heritable.* In other words, when we look at human variance in spirituality, a person's degree of spirituality is determined 29 percent by heredity, and 71 percent by environment. Our spirituality is substantially—roughly two-thirds—a factor of how we're raised, the company we keep, the things we do to build the muscle. But still a significant degree of our capacity to experience the sacred and transcendent—one-third—is inscribed in our genetic code, as innate as our eye color or fingerprints.[47]

This is a striking finding. Let us proclaim the one true God and teach our children to do the same. After all, we were created to do so!

---

47. Lisa Miller, PhD, *The Awakened Brain: The New Science of Spirituality and Our Quest for an Inspired Life* (New York: Penguin Random House, LLC, 2021), 57–58.

YOU ARE THEIR FIRST TEACHER

Whether homeschooling or not, parents are their children's most impactful teachers, and our goal as Christians is to influence our children to have a lifelong love for the Lord and serve others. When I was raising my children, I had no formal training on how to be a parent *and* a teacher, yet I had to learn to be both. I needed to be able to effectively deliver information in a way that would be best received by my child, who was also my student. Nineteenth-century educator John Milton Gregory wrote:

> It's the teacher's mission...by sympathy, by example, and by every means of influence—by objects for the senses, by facts for the intelligence—to excite the mind of the pupils, to stimulate their thoughts...The greatest of teachers say: "The seed is the Word." The true teacher stirs the ground and sows the seed.[48]

Some have a natural talent for teaching or speaking to an audience, so they can be very effectual. But me? I had to learn—and I am still learning. Aristotle wrote something that I think applies to teachers, speakers, and parents. He said that to be an effective speaker, one needs to incorporate three things that will connect the heart, emotion, and intellect of the listener: *ethos, pathos,* and *logos*.

Ethos or "ethics" is the person's character, which must be trustworthy. If the character is flawed or untrustworthy, then the child will be suspicious of the message. I had a friend whose father was an alcoholic and often lied. My friend told me she didn't trust a thing her dad said. How sad! If a child can't trust a parent, who can they trust?

---

48. Hendricks, *Teaching to Change Lives*, 68.

Pathos or "emotion" is the persuasion or delivery of the message. We need to have right motives behind our words. Deceptive persuasion can cause children to be skeptical about what they're hearing. Some parents think it is okay to trick or slightly deceive their children because they believe it will benefit them in the long run. Such parents will say or do whatever it takes to get their children to listen. For instance, they may give their children false promises, tell lies to scare them, or cry fake tears, believing the ends justify the means. This is consequentialism, and the end result is that the child will learn not to trust the parent.

Logos is the "logic" or reasoning of the message. Children can be very astute. If what is being taught doesn't seem logical, they may become skeptical of situations and people. Unbelief and doubt may cause them to question future directives.

Spiritually healthy families will impact their children's spiritual health in the long run. Faith-sharing parents raise faith-sharing children. The word *inspiration* means "a divine influence or action on a person believed to qualify him or her to receive and communicate sacred revelation."[49] Parents who exhibit inspiration, imagination, and creativity help their children acquire a deep desire to learn about Jesus and make Him the desire of their hearts.

---

49. *Merriam-Webster Dictionary*, s.v. "Inspiration," www.merriam-webster.com/dictionary/inspiration.

7

PRACTICAL METHODS FOR CONNECTING CHILDREN TO JESUS

A Sunday school teacher who was teaching a group of kindergarteners had the class sing "Jesus Loves Me" because that song went well with the day's lesson. When they finished singing, a little boy raised his hand.

"What does 'sino' mean?" he asked.

Perplexed, the teacher asked the boy to repeat himself. "What does 'sino' mean? You know, in the song, we sing, 'Jesus loves me, this sino.'"

The teacher struggled not to laugh as realization dawned on her. Slowly, she sang the line back to the boy, enunciating clearly, "This. I. Know."

Instilling and modeling biblical truth can be done—with lots of patience, proper enunciation, and, when you have small children, a few laughs. Perhaps you have heard some of the cute things children say when they say their prayers or recall biblical stories. There's the child who prayed, "And forgive us our trash baskets as we forgive those who put trash in our baskets."[50] Or the child who

---

50. "Church Kids Say the Darndest Things," David Van Alstyne blog, davidvanalstyne.com/pg-kidschurchsay.html.

said, "The greatest miracle in the Bible is when Joshua told his son to stand still and he obeyed him."[51]

While their interpretation of biblical stories can be comical, it is important that we make certain they fully understand what God is trying to tell us. Even though they are young, they are capable of accurately learning God's Word.

CAN WE TEACH LITTLE ONES?

Is it possible to teach biblical truths to toddlers and preschoolers and have them understand the concepts? Yes, it is! So how can children be taught to love Jesus with all their heart and mind? Can they truly grasp who Jesus is?

Jesus said, *"Let the little children come to me and do not hinder them"* (Matthew 19:14). He also said, *"Truly I tell you, anyone who will not receive the kingdom of God like a little child will never enter it"* (Mark 10:15).

Jesus was referring to infants and toddlers. The word *babies* comes from the Greek word *brephos*, which refers to children as young as eight days after birth.[52] The Psalms tell us the importance of our little ones:

> *Through the praise of children and infants you have established a stronghold against your enemies, to silence the foe and the avenger.* (Psalm 8:2)

> *Yet you desired faithfulness even in the womb; you taught me wisdom in that secret place.* (Psalm 51:6)

---

51. Ibid.
52. Morgenthaler, *Right from the Start*, 25.

The authors of *Children Matter* state, "We might think of a child's belief and love for Jesus as the embryo of faith, a most crucial reality, a beginning but real relationship with God."[53]

Interacting with our little ones can bring us great joy. Try to voice biblical words and phrases during your everyday routines and sing songs about Jesus. Children love to repeat our words, and it helps them learn to speak.

A fun and effective way to help your little ones remember Bible verses and worship songs is to incorporate them into your daily routine. Sing Scripture verses to their favorite tunes while in the car with your child. Talk about things like the fruit of the Spirit at mealtimes. At bedtime, ask your son or daughter what blessings they saw God give to them or someone else that day. When thinking about God and the wisdom in His Word is part of a child's daily routine, that routine will carry on into adulthood.

Dependable, godly parents are those who purposefully, continually, and lovingly instill godly doctrine. Those efforts create a deep desire for Jesus within their children's hearts and minds. In the last chapter, I list some fun activities that can effectively teach children about Jesus.

FAMILY INFLUENCE IS STRONG

Have you ever heard your exact words come out of your child's mouth with the same expression on their face and the same body language? Sometimes it's just so cute...but at other times, it can be downright humiliating.

There's a common saying, "More is caught than taught." Children learn by observing their environment and other people. What goes on in the home—peace or chaos, faith or doubt—will

---

53. Scottie May, et al., *Children Matter: Celebrating Their Place in the Church, Family, and Community* (Grand Rapids, MI: Wm. B. Eerdmans Publishing Co., 2005), 51.

be part of a child's learning and understanding. Dr. Kathy Koch states, "Even the best ideas implemented faithfully will not result in consistent positive change if [our] character is not transformed. Transformation happens as character is caught and taught."[54]

We know some days don't go as planned. There are moments of anger, sadness, and stress when faced with an illness, death, insufficient money, or any negative life issue. Our children are watching closely to see how we act and react. During these difficult situations, do we edify others, or do we lose our temper and gossip? Do our children see us taking a break to calm down and pray to the Father?

As you try to model a godly example for your children, ask Jesus for strength, patience, love, and all the fruit of His Holy Spirit. Children reflect what you say and do. Psychologist Lev Vygotsky said young children will learn faster when they witness someone who is older and has mastered a skill that the child is trying to learn.[55] This is why children with older siblings can learn at a faster rate than children who have no siblings or only younger ones.

Seek out an older Christian mom as a mentor because more than likely, they've *been there and done that* and are full of wisdom to share. (See Titus 2:3–5.) Ask any mother of grown children how short time felt while their children were going through their life phases. Seeing the whirling hour hand of life's clock is a reminder to capture those precious moments that blossom and an invitation to show and speak about Jesus's teachings, blessings, and love.

LET'S PLAN FOR SUCCESS

Some of us like to do things with our children on the spur of the moment, while others like to plan ahead. While doing

---

54. Koch, *Start with the Heart*, 33.
55. Saul McLeod, "Vygotsky's Zone of Proximal Development and Scaffolding," *Simply Psychology*, May 14, 2023, www.simplypsychology.org/Zone-of-Proximal-Development.html.

something spontaneous can be surprising and fun, there are times when planning is needed to ensure experiences that produce knowledge, wisdom, and order. Being prepared by knowing the next step helps to bring about a positive outcome.

What outcomes do we want in our lifetime—both for us and for our children? Good results rarely just happen. We need preparation and resources to help us make wise decisions regarding careers, where we will live, vacations, and, most importantly, how to raise our children. Dr. George Barna states, "Every respectable military strategist, educator, business manager, political leader, and *effective parent* will agree that achieving positive outcomes rarely happens by chance. It is almost always the result of good planning and diligent implementation" (emphasis mine).[56]

One of the most important decisions parents will make is how to raise their children to become strong, Bible-based disciples of Jesus. Formulating and sticking to a plan will be easier when God's Word becomes the foundation. The Bible contains specific directives and guidelines that can be understood with Holy Spirit-instilled wisdom.

Parents often find themselves at opposite ends of the *how to raise my kids* spectrum. Mom and Dad may have very different priorities and ideas about how their faith impacts decisions. It's essential to have a list of nonnegotiables—things that shifting circumstances should have minimal or no impact on. Things like praying for and with your children, regularly attending church with them, and pointing to the Bible for wisdom should be on that list.

Children are God's most precious gifts to us. Parents must work together to help mold their young hearts to obtain a love for Jesus that's more significant than any other love, even the love they have for us. Jesus must hold first place in their hearts, not second or third. Our spiritual heart bears witness to what we desire most,

---

56. George Barna, *Revolutionary Parenting: What the Research Shows Really Works* (Carol Stream, IL: Tyndale 2007), 40.

our minds reflect what we know to be true or false, and our soul reveals who we truly are. Jesus wants His children to love Him with all their hearts, minds, and souls. When children seek Jesus with all their hearts, first and foremost, they will take responsibility for their godly character with some encouragement.

Whole Heart Ministries founder Sally Clarkson believes:

> Training in character gives our children the foundation of internal strength to learn responsibility and the motivation to be able to do what God has prepared them to do in life. To focus merely on knowledge without laying a foundation of character makes education limited and without purpose. Training children to grow the muscle of character prepares them to be able to apply the knowledge, skills, and wisdom they have learned in practical ways.[57]

SHOW AND TALK ABOUT JESUS

When I was a child, I loved show-and-tell. Once a week, we were allowed to bring in one item to show our classmates and tell why it was important to us. I once brought in my little book of easy-to-read prayers with illustrations. It was special to me because I would read one prayer each night before I went to sleep, which made me feel safe and secure.

It's wonderful to hear parents talk to their children about Jesus openly and frequently. I love to visit families whose homes are decorated with plaques, sayings, and pictures that reflect biblical principles. Their homes become places of show-and-tell, and I can feel the presence of the Holy Spirit there. What their children see will be engrained in their minds. Regarding God's commands,

---

57. Sally Clarkson, *Awaking Wonder: Opening Your Child's Heart to the Beauty of Learning* (Bloomington, IN: Bethany House Publishers, 2020), 139.

Scripture tells us, *"Write them on the doorframes of your houses and on your gates"* (Deuteronomy 11:20).

When my husband and I built our home, I placed a Bible and a cross in a plastic bag where the front door entrance would stand before the concrete foundation was laid. This way, our home would be built upon the foundation of the Word of God, spiritually and literally. We also have Scriptures throughout our house, serving as visual reminders that this is a home that honors God.

The Watermark Gospel (www.watermarkgospel.com) is a wonderful resource to help you show and talk about Jesus and discover Him throughout the Bible, from Genesis to Revelation. The whole family will enjoy the animations and other resources that show how the heroes and heroines of Scripture really point us to our one true hero, Jesus, and His great triumph over death!

8

CULTIVATING TRUST IN GOD AND PARENTAL GUIDANCE

To this day, I still recall my mother's little sayings: "Money doesn't grow on trees," "Because I said so," and "Don't forget to pray!" Maybe you heard some similar sayings in your own family. These often stick in a child's mind into adulthood.

Repetition can help to teach your children truths about God and His Word that they can carry with them throughout their lives. One of the easiest ways to help young children trust the Lord is to teach them to recite simple prayers and phrases, such as "God is good," "Jesus loves me all the time," "Thank You, Jesus, for taking care of me," or, "I love You, Jesus," just to name a few.

These prayers will saturate your child's heart, soul, and mind as they learn to love and trust God. This helps to *prepare the soil* early so the *seeds of godly wisdom can be planted* into fertile ground later.

However, these teaching moments and methods can be disrupted if children have fears that are either real or imaginary. Fear can become a detriment to learning and retaining what is being taught. Children can be afraid of things that they see or hear, as well as things that their imagination conjures up. Consider this acronym for FEAR: False Evidence Appearing Real.

We are born with a fear of loud noises and a fear of falling. Other fears are learned from life experiences; fear from loss, for example, can occur after a divorce, the death of a family member or pet, the loss of a favorite toy or blanket, or a friend moving away. Separation anxiety is very common among young children and can instill great fear as well as fear of worldly conflict and natural disasters. Many children are diagnosed each year with some type of clinical anxiety. And teenagers worry about peer pressure, getting a job, or attending college. Learning to trust in the Lord will bring peace when fear creeps in to steal their joy.

EVIL INFLUENCES CAN CAUSE GREAT FEAR

First and foremost, our homes should be havens from an evil world. It's important not to permit anything that could give Satan a foothold, such as violent video games or inappropriate toys. Toys and game that depict violence, promote aggression, or embody negative characteristics can become entranceways for the evil one.

Children have always been and will continue to be the devil's main target. In Mark 9, we read about a boy who had been tortured by an evil spirit since childhood. The boy's father told Jesus, *"It has often thrown him into fire or water to kill him. But if you can do anything, take pity on us and help us"* (Mark 9:22). Jesus said, *"'If you can?'...Everything is possible for one who believes"* (verse 23). The father exclaimed, *"I do believe; help me overcome my unbelief!"* (verse 24).

Get to know the parents of your children's friends. Make sure that they don't allow violent or evil games, toys, and movies in their household. That being said, our children need to know that there is evil in the world. Otherwise, they will not have a complete picture of God's saving grace. When my children were little, I gave them a spray bottle of water and told them that if they woke up scared because they thought there were monsters in their room, they should say, "All monsters, be gone in the name of Jesus," and then spray some water as they claimed His name. Poof! All the monsters disappeared. This encourages children to speak the powerful name of Jesus over the physical spaces they're in from a young age. It worked for my kids.

GOD IS TRUSTWORTHY

When I was nine years old, I would crawl into my mother's bed whenever I heard noises outside my bedroom window. The noise turned out to be a tree branch scraping the window when the wind blew. Discovering the cause of that scraping sound and praying to Jesus for faith gave me the courage to sleep in my own bed.

Fear interferes with children's feelings of security and safety. When they learn the truth about what's causing their fears and know that their parents and the Lord can protect them, those fears diminish and no longer hold them captive. Their minds will then be free to learn about Jesus.

My friend's little grandson tends to worry. He is what she calls "a thinker who overanalyzes a lot!" Whether it's about friends at school, trying a new activity, sleeping in his room, or misplacing a favorite toy, he seems to navigate life with an undercurrent of anxiety. Some children are prone to fear, anxiety, or worry. We can help them conquer these feelings by first acknowledging them rather than dismissing or belittling them. Even as adults, we can experience many different types of phobias or irrational fears. For example, eisoptrophobia is a fear of mirrors, and ombrophobia is a fear of rain. Others may not understand these fears, but that doesn't lessen them.

When engaged in conversation with a child who is fearful or anxious, be at eye level with them, use a calm voice, acknowledge their fear, and pray with them. Anxiety or fear is an opportunity to show children the importance and power of prayer. Explain that

God is more powerful than anything else, so they can trust Him always.

I love this quote from the late Jennifer Kennedy Dean, former executive director of the Praying Life Foundation:

> Prayer is not a way for you to influence God but a way for God to influence you…Prayer is not a duty to perform, or simply a discipline to engage in, but rather prayer becomes the breath of my soul.[58]

Roleplay and reverse roleplay are excellent tools to help children and teens learn to confront their fears and how to act or react during fearful situations. Playing with puppets is an excellent tool to use for roleplay for younger children.

There are more than four hundred Bible verses that talk about fear or anxiety. Select one each day to read with your children. Here are a few:

> *Be strong and courageous. Do not be afraid; do not be discouraged, for the* Lord *your God will be with you wherever you go.* (Joshua 1:9)

> *For I am the* Lord *your God who takes hold of your right hand and says to you, Do not fear; I will help you.* (Isaiah 41:13)

---

58. Jennifer Kennedy Dean, *Seek: 28 Days to Extraordinary Prayer* (Birmingham, AL: New Hope Publishers, 2019), 7, 9.

Do not be anxious about anything, but in every situation, by prayer and petition, with thanksgiving, present your requests to God. And the peace of God, which transcends all understanding, will guard your hearts and your minds in Christ Jesus. (Philippians 4:6–7)

Cast all your anxiety on him because he cares for you.
(1 Peter 5:7)

LOVE AND KNOWLEDGE

One of the best ways we can help our children navigate fear is to remind them that they are loved and secure in that love. Simple things like leaving notes in their backpacks to remind them that they are loved, or texting a verse or word of encouragement from the Bible to the older kids are positive ways to start their day. Besides lots of hugs and kisses, there are many ways to demonstrate love and care for your children that will help them feel good about themselves, conquer fear, and learn to love others. Love builds trust!

You can write loving notes and place them in their lunchbox or send them a card in the mail. Children love getting an envelope from the mailbox that is addressed to them! Send a love note from Jesus, using His words from the Bible.

Ask open-ended questions about their day at school, play dates, or other occasions. Questions such as, "Did you see someone being kind today? What did they do?" or "How did you show kindness today?" or "Did you talk to Jesus today? What did you say?" give you an opportunity to express love and concern. They also teach your children how to ask questions that promote beneficial dialogue.

Also, if your children ask a question out of the blue, and you're not sure why, gently ask them to explain. You may find another question behind that question. For example, if your child asks, "Why do people die?" they may be wondering why God allowed their uncle to die after they prayed for God to heal him. Be honest with your answers to build trust between you, your child, and God. Never lie and try not to break a promise to your children. They desire and deserve honesty and loyalty from you. They may become fearful when they learn they cannot trust their parents.

Take the time to listen to the insignificant issues now, and they will want to share their significant issues as they get older. Always give full attention when listening to what they are saying and remain at eye level for little ones. Make sure that they trust you are hearing what they are saying. Strong relationships start with being mutually responsive. Always listen to their point of view and model how to disagree without being disagreeable.

Give your children more yeses, less nos, and minimize the maybes. Dr. Lise Eliot, a research neuroscientist, found that children who were frequently spoken to using negative words and phrases such as *don't*, *no*, and *stop it* had poorer speaking skills than those who were given fewer negative responses.[59]

Smile often, hold hands often, pray often, and be the last to let go of an embrace. Tell your children a hundred times a day that they are loved. And remind them often to pray every day. I still tell my adult children that I love them and remind them to say their prayers.

Help and guide them to do their tasks with love and patience. Encourage and teach but let them complete the task on their own. That's how they learn, grow, and become independent and critical thinkers. If you do everything for your children, they may feel that you don't have faith in them to complete the task successfully.

59. Dr. Lise Eliot, *What's Going on in There? How the Brain and Mind Develop in the First Five Years of Life* (New York: Bantam Books, 1999), 383.

At dinnertime, teach your children good table manners, ask questions, and listen. Show interest in what they say by having a positive conversation. Making dinnertime fun helps to form a bond that helps children make better choices now and in the future. It will also prepare them to withstand negative influences from others and culture.

Because of their innocence, children can learn to trust God and be a witness of faith in Jesus. While the Bible doesn't specifically say Jesus laughed, I believe He did so when children played at His feet. Children have a great curiosity, and they marvel at His creation rather than taking it for granted as adults sometimes do.

SIMPLICITY OF LIFE

We are called to live a simple life like Jesus. He did not own any earthly possessions yet He owned everything. Simplicity is a virtue. Jesus tells us, *"Watch out! Be on your guard against all kinds of greed; life does not consist in an abundance of possessions"* (Luke 12:15). Limiting the number of our possessions, media time, or social obligations allows us to find the freedom to live joyfully with our children and teach them that what matters most is spending time with each other and with the Lord.

Take time to write down how you spend your time and money, and how you can make some changes to simplify your life. You will find freedom, peace, and time to wonder at God's creations with your children.

As Bible teacher and naturalist Eryn Lynum notes:

God placed curiosity in your children's minds and spirits to compel them in their pursuit of him. If nature is where we find him, then curiosity is the compass guiding us.[60]

---

60. Lynum, *Rooted in Wonder*, 90.

Simplifying our lives allows us to live like children—carefree, full of wonder, and dependent upon our Father. Jesus says, *"Truly I tell you, unless you change and become like little children, you will never enter the kingdom of heaven"* (Matthew 18:3). Children learn to trust God as they see the evidence of His creation, witness His Word as truth, and have parents who emulate His character.

9

HELPING TO SHAPE
A GODLY WORLDVIEW

When my children were little, my husband Guy and I would load up our van with books, summer homework, snacks, and movies and drive from Florida to Michigan to spend the summer with Grandma, Grandpa, and the rest of the family. During this long drive, my children would ask me to read my *Sea Kids* stories to them again and again. These stories helped to shape their worldview as they learned how to be kind and loving, pray, and give thanks to Jesus. I am happy that all seven of my *Sea Kids* books are very popular among parents and their children, and our animated series can now be seen on Right Now Media, Pure Flix, Answers. TV, and other streaming venues.

Dr. George Barna states that a child's worldview starts to formulate around the age of fifteen months and is formed by age thirteen.[61] Since their worldview is shaped in such a short time, we should use every moment to guide our children and lead them to truth.

Are we instilling secular worldviews or godly ones? How can we teach the Word of God lovingly and organically so that our children will learn and retain it?

One way is to start early by linking words to their emotions. For example, six-month-old babies love to look at their reflection

---

61. Barna, *Raising Spiritual Champions*, 6-7.

in a mirror. When they smile at themselves, tell them, "Jesus loves you!" They should hear the name of Jesus more than any other name. You are connecting their happy emotion with the name of Jesus. This is preparing the soil of their hearts to become fertile so that when spiritual *seeds are planted* later, they *"produce a crop— some thirty, some sixty, some a hundred times what was sown"* (Mark 4:20). There is much more you can do to help your children obtain a godly worldview.

Ministry leader Josh Mulvihill wisely points out:

> Worldly influence in the hearts of our children is hard to detect, because it takes time for weeds to grow. With God's grace and proper training, our children can be Bible-believing Christians who are spiritual salmon, swimming against the current of culture.[62]

THE MOMENTS AFTER BIRTH

Words didn't adequately describe my feelings when I first held my son. As I mentioned in my introduction, I thanked Jesus and was amazed at the size of my infant's hands. Knowing what I know now, I wish I had also whispered into my son's ear, "Jesus loves you."

When God blesses you with a bundle of joy, let the first words your baby hears be, "Jesus loves you."

Muslims start to instill their worldview in their children imme-diately after birth. The father whispers the *Hadīth* in the infant's right ear: "God is great, there is no God but Allah. Muhammad is the messenger of Allah. Come to prayer." This devotion to Allah and Islamic traditions starts with occasional prayers and continues

62. Josh Mulvihill, *Preparing Children for Marriage: How to Teach God's Good Design for Marriage, Sex, Purity, and Dating* (Phillipsburg, NJ: P&R Publishing, 2017), 33.

with elaborate daily rituals. If they can raise up children for Allah, we can raise up disciples who exhibit love for Christ.

TEACHING BIBLICAL WISDOM WHILE HAVING FUN

Homeschool parents are always seeking fun, creative ways to incorporate Bible teachings into their lesson plans. How to impart the truth of Scripture in interesting and engaging ways is a challenge we all face as we strive to raise our children to have a lifelong, unshakable faith and a biblical worldview. Teaching children to memorize Scripture in Sunday school and at home helps them become more Christlike. The good news is there are many ways to incorporate biblical doctrine.

At ages two and three, children rarely ask questions about Jesus. They simply listen to what is being taught about Him. They want to mimic you when you pray, and they want to repeat what you say. When you are at a child's birthday party, after singing, "Happy Birthday," say, "Jesus loves birthday parties, don't you?" When you're at the zoo, tell them, "Jesus made the tiger so big and strong!" At the grocery store, say, "Jesus wants us to eat healthy food." You get the idea. Say His name often and acknowledge Him in all you do. This is how we fulfill the directives given in the *Shema* in Deuteronomy 6.

Bibles for toddlers are excellent tools for introducing biblical stories. Many little ones who have not yet learned to read can finger-follow the words on the pages as they repeat what they hear. Be sure to point out how awesome Jesus is in everything that He did. You can say things like, "Jesus walked on water—isn't that amazing?!"

Children also love repetitive stories. Education professor Robert J. Keely says, "When we turn Bible stories into moral tales for small children, we realize that, at best, we are hoping to influence their most basic instincts and convince them that it is in their best interest to be 'good.' [However,] influencing moral behavior is not the same as building faith."[63] When reading a Bible story, look for the faith lesson *and* a moral lesson. A faith lesson reflects on Jesus within the story, while a moral lesson teaches how Jesus acted. We learn from His character and His behavior.[64]

Faith and moral lessons solidify a cohesive, effective foundation for faith formation, moral attitudes, and moral behaviors. Biblical faith formation is essential for obtaining a Christian worldview. It is acquired through various experiences that nurture a solid transformation by which faith in God is accomplished, cherished, and then flourishes.

When I was little, one of my favorite things to do was walk to the library with my mother. We couldn't afford to purchase books, but I was so happy to bring library books home, even knowing I had to return them. Raising children to love reading is one of the best gifts we can give them.

Literacy expert Dr. J. Richard Gentry says:

Spending time reading and talking to your baby pays dividends. When you read aloud to your baby with positive conversational interchanges you engender long-term gains and increase your baby's or toddler's intelligence... One remarkable finding with important implications for parenting was that positive verbal responses—praise as opposed to negative conversational feedback—resulted in better intellectual and literacy gains.[65]

---

63. Keeley, *Helping Our Children Grow in Faith*, 84.
64. Ibid., 90.
65. Dr. J. Richard Gentry, *Raising Confident Readers: How to Teach Your Child to Read and Write—from Baby to Age 7* (Cambridge, MA: Da Capo Press, 2010), 3–4.

Studies show that even eight-month-old babies can recognize and remember specific storybook words for up to two weeks after hearing them repeatedly. Gentry says the very early years are part of "the longest phase, perhaps the easiest time for teaching reading, and maybe the most important one in terms of its impact on your child's intelligence and future academic success."[66]

When reading Bible stories to wee little ones, simply use words they understand. Use concrete terms to describe God as our Creator, for example, saying something like, "God made the sun, water, and trees," or "God made your eyes, your nose, and your smile."

As children get older, reading will keep their memories sharp and help them think strategically as they anticipate what will happen next in the material. They love routine, and reading can be a daily one they will look forward to.

Help your children understand that the Bible is truth, and there is no other book like it. Give them examples of what is true and what is false so they can understand the meaning of the word *true*. For example, ask them, "It is true that the grass is green? Or is it true that the grass is blue?" This will ensure that they understand what the word *true* means.

When reading a biblical story, be expressive and use props. My children's book series, *Sea Kids*, is featured on a free app called Novel Effect. It's a great tool that enhances reading time by bringing the stories to life as your device syncs the background music, sound effects, and character voices to the spoken words on each page. It magnifies the story being read, and the app has many books from which to choose. In my book, *I'm Not Afraid!*, which deals with fear, Susie is afraid of roller coasters. As the story is read, the children can hear the roller coaster, children laughing,

---

66. Ibid., 67.

balloons popping, and all the fun sounds of an amusement park.[67] Children love triggering sound effects with their voices, which encourages them to read.

USING BIBLICAL WORDS

I loved going to Sunday school as a child. I had so much fun learning about God and doing arts and crafts. I still remember the cross I made from bird seed and popsicle sticks, which I was eager to show to my mother. That was also the day I learned meaning of the word crucifixion. As I walked home, I held it tightly in my tiny hand—so tightly that many seeds had fallen off by the time I got home. But my mother helped me to glue more seeds back on that cross.

Young children can learn about Jesus's miracles, that He is God's only Son, and about His crucifixion, death, and resurrection. They should also learn words like *sin, salvation, prayer, repenting, worship, praise,* and *communion,* among others. It is best to use these words and help our children understand their meanings, as we never know when a child will grasp a biblical concept.

Josh Mulvihill asks:

> Could it be that one reason young people are doctrinally ignorant, spiritually confused, and living with a syncretistic faith system is that we have reduced our teaching to the couple dozen moralistic stories found in most children's Bibles? Our children need the soul-gripping, life-altering, meat-based, Jesus-centered teachings of God's Word.[68]

It's interesting to note that farmers plant corn early in the season to inhibit the growth of weeds and reduce insect infestation. We do

---

67. Novel Effect Reading of *Sea Kids* book, *I'm Not Afraid!*, www.youtube.com/watch?v=PiaN6VoSIVs; also see raisingchristiankids.com.
68. Mulvihill, *Preparing Children for Marriage,* 40.

the same by *preparing the soil* and *planting spiritual seeds* early in an effort to reduce the infestation of doubt, confusion, and unbelief in our children. Start reading Bible stories and using biblical words early and often to infuse godly doctrine and mold their Christian worldview. Also make sure your child understands the meaning of each word in the Bible verse that they are reading or memorizing.

THE GREATEST TEACHERS

I have fond memories of my first-grade teacher, Mrs. Paulson, who would read a story as if she were putting on a Broadway show. She made the stories come to life, entertaining the class while teaching.

We are so blessed to have the greatest teacher, Jesus, who taught us with His parables. When reading stories from the Bible, act out some of the characters by using fun and maybe even silly voices. No one at any age wants to listen to a story that is read in a monotone voice.

The authors of *Listening to Children on the Spiritual Journey* say:

> It is important to note that how we tell the story makes a difference in the God our children meet; our view of God colors the God we portray in the story...The story-teller's preparation enhances that engagement. The adult reading or telling a story prepares in advance by seeking to enter the story, experience the thoughts and feelings of the characters and the wonder of God's presence and actions. Then those feelings—that wonder, awe, and sense of mystery—can come through in the voice of the storyteller, aiding God's word to grasp the heart of the child.[69]

69. Catherine Stonehouse and Scottie May, *Listening to Children on the Spiritual Journey: Guidance for Those Who Teach and Nurture* (Grand Rapids, MI: Baker Publishing Group, 2010), 85–86.

The tone of voice you use will change how the story is perceived. For example, when Peter floundered as he tried to walk on water toward Jesus (see Matthew 14:29–30), did the Lord talk to him in a stern tone or a loving voice when He asked, "*O you of little faith, why did you doubt?*" (verse 31 ESV). Try both. You will see a difference.

Children will likely remember something important or want to obey their parents' rules when creative word pictures are used. Good word pictures can elicit emotions that make the story come to life. For instance, if I wanted my child to remember to brush her teeth every night, I would tell her this story:

> Once there was a little boy who never wanted to brush his teeth. Because he didn't brush his teeth, his teeth were dirty, and his breath smelled like a garbage can. He asked his mommy why the children didn't want to play with him, and she told him it was because he never brushed his teeth. It made him sad so he decided he would brush his teeth every morning and every night. After a while, his teeth became white as snow, and he no longer had stinky breath! He found out that he liked peppermint toothpaste but, most important, his friends now enjoyed playing with him.

When my children were little, we read about eight to ten Christian picture books each night. We would first pray that Jesus would teach and guide us. Then I would point out things in the pictures to help them comprehend and remember the message. When possible, I would read the same story in the morning and again before they went to bed. After we finished reading, we would thank Jesus for the story. Sometimes I would read the same book every day for many days. Children love repetition, and it helps them to retain what they learn.

INCORPORATING TOYS

Including toys in children's reading and playtime makes these moments fun and more meaningful. Acting out a story with stuffed animals, puppets, dolls, or toys like miniature cars can make the story come alive. That car can help little ones flee sin. A baby doll can be a stand-in for baby Jesus. Acting out the biblical story demonstrates that *"the word of God is alive and active"* (Hebrews 4:12).

The first three years of a child's life are vitally important for their development. This is the time to encourage them and help them learn new tasks. Choose toys and activities that will challenge them without frustrating them. Rotate toys from ones they see often to those that have been put away for a while. My children loved it when we dug out a toy that they had not seen in a few months. They would yell, "Wow! I love that toy! Remember this one, Mommy?"

Each week, choose a biblical theme that you can reinforce in song, play, and prayer. Help your children act out a Bible story using puppets, costumes, and toys. Record them teaching godly principles to their dolls or action figures or to you. Children love to see and hear themselves; when they *teach*, it helps them to retain what they have learned.

SPIRITUAL PLAYROOMS

I loved walking into my daughter's room and finding her having a tea party with her dolls. I would stand back and listen to her adorable conversations. One day, I remember her saying, "No, don't eat that cookie before we pway!" She was so cute, even though her sharp tone was a little bit too reflective of what she obviously heard from me.

If you are able, set up a playroom that has various stations, each of which incorporates Jesus or biblical principles. For example, purchase biblical Legos, fruit of the Spirit puzzles, and dolls or puppets that all represent Christian values and morals. Have a center for Christian-themed arts and crafts, Christian books to read, church and prayer items, and costumes for dress up, such as Moses, Sarah, Abraham, John the Baptist, Mary, Jesus, or any other biblical character. A place to *play church* is important. We want to help our children experience God during playtime.

I was raised Catholic, and the scent of incense during Mass not only smelled wonderful, it was a mysterious and spiritual element for me as a child. Engage your children's senses during playtime—sight, taste, sound, smell, and touch. Play Christian children's songs in the background as they play to make this a sacred time that incorporates fun. If there's no fun, you might hear the dreaded phrase all parents despise: "I'm bored." Children learn best while having fun, but if they're bored, don't always rush in with ideas about what to do next. Boredom can be an opportunity for children to contemplate on their own and nourish their creativity.

FUN WAYS TO LIVE BIBLICALLY

Living out biblical principles will help your child obtain a Christian worldview. As a family, you can volunteer at church or school to help everyone stay connected to the body of Christ. To teach the meaning of good stewardship, you can volunteer at a local animal shelter or a nonprofit organization that helps and clothes those in need. Remind your child, *"The King will reply, 'Truly I tell you, whatever you did for one of the least of these brothers and sisters of mine, you did for me'"* (Matthew 25:40). You can also volunteer at a homeless shelter or a nursing home. These residents love to see the smiling faces of little children! Pray and ask God to show you where your family can serve Him and others well.

My children used to love playing in the mud; perhaps yours do too. Have a family foot-washing ceremony when your children come home with dirty feet. Teach them how to be servants like Jesus, explaining that Jesus washed the apostles' feet.

Make sure to spend quality time with grandparents who have lived godly lives and have much wisdom and love to share. My children also enjoyed extended family gatherings, so we would plan get-togethers often. The book *Cousin Camp*[70] offers great suggestions for connecting grandparents with grandchildren and kids having fun with their cousins, thus uniting an extended family. Julie Lavendar's book *365 Ways to Love Your Child*[71] is another excellent resource for family time fun.

Here are some other ways to show the love of Christ to others:

+ Help an elderly neighbor. Older children can cut their grass, and younger children can bring them flowers. My children would play the piano for our elderly neighbors, which brought so much joy to them. My now-adult children still remember these special moments.

+ Bake cookies for police officers and firefighters and make homemade thank-you notes. This will help children learn to respect and appreciate authority.

+ Have your children choose some clothes and toys to donate to charity. Make sure to tell them that for it to truly be a sacrifice, they need to give away one thing they like. We are to give in obedience, not abundance, just like the widow's offering. (See Mark 12:43–44.)

+ Create care packages for homeless families. If your family is able, when you purchase *buy one, get one free* items, give one away.

70. Susan Alexander Yates, *Cousin Camp: A Grandparent's Guide to Creating Fun, Faith, and Memories That Last* (Grand Rapids, MI: Revell, 2020).
71. Julie Lavender, *365 Ways to Love Your Child: Turning Little Moments into Lasting Memories* (Grand Rapids, MI: Revell, 2020).

+ Older children can offer to babysit for free or be a mother's helper for a mother who desperately needs help.

These are just a few examples of activities that help to instill the characteristics of Christ. Let's be doers of the Word by exhibiting our hearts of faith in our lives.

ONE-ON-ONE TIME AND FAMILY TIME

One-on-one time with your little one is the best faith gift you can give! Remember the maxim, "Yesterday is history, tomorrow is a mystery, today is a gift, that's why it's called the present." Be present and become *a present* as you give your undivided attention to your child. When it comes to raising the next generation to honor and love the Lord, the most essential factor and influence on children is a faithful relationship with their parents.

Establish a set time for family worship, reading the Bible, and devotions. Be sure to offer discussion and application questions during the reading and afterward, such as, "Does this story remind you of anything or someone?" or "How do you think that character was feeling when that happened?" or "What lesson we can learn from this story?" Here are six types of questions to ask:

+ Knowledge questions—"How many gifts did the kings bring to baby Jesus?"

+ Comprehension questions—"What do all these stories have to do with each other?"

+ Application questions—"How can praying to the Holy Spirit help you when you are afraid of the dark?"

+ Analysis questions—"Why did Moses's mother place him in the river?"

+ Synthesis questions—"What do you think would have happened if Moses didn't listen to the burning bush?"

+ Evaluation questions—"Do you think it is good to pray more than once a day?"

Asking questions helps to enhance children's critical and reflective thinking skills, expands vocabulary and language skills, helps children to develop social skills, encourages a desire to be curious and gain a love for learning, fosters confidence as they contribute to the discussion, stimulates emotional awareness as they notice how they feel, strengthens the bond between parent and child, and helps to build a strong Christian worldview.

10

WHY DO WE BELIEVE WHAT WE BELIEVE?

We all know smart people who are avid readers and nearly obsessive learners. They are often eager to share what they know. But sometimes, these very intelligent individuals have trouble in how they express and share information. They may sound harsh or arrogant and appear to have no interest in what their listener has to say. They may be accurate in their facts, but their tone and delivery block others from hearing what they are conveying.

Have you ever felt so strongly about something that you absolutely had to defend it when someone spoke against it? How did you proceed? I have remained in heated debates when something was important to me, and my tone reflected my anger. As a result, the other person only heard my anger, not my valid points.

I remember reading Dale Carnegie's popular book, *How to Win Friends & Influence People*.[72] Carnegie said that when people are more interested in winning an argument and approach a discussion rudely, the other person metaphorically puts their hands up to fight. However, if we act politely, they are more likely to react in the same manner so that a civil dialogue can follow. Apologetics is mastered in the same way.

---

72. Dale Carnegie, *How to Win Friends & Influence People* (New York: Pocket Books, 1998).

WHAT IS APOLOGETICS?

Apologetics comes from the ancient Greek word *apologia*, which means "a verbal defense." Apologetics does not mean we're apologizing for what we believe. It means we are defending what we believe and why, building a *reasoned defense* for divinely revealed facts. Some truths—such as the divinity of Jesus or biblical miracles—cannot be fully expressed by reasoning or experimental methods. Their validity must be defended in a nonconfrontational way. C. S. Lewis believed that imagination and reasoning work together and are not mutually exclusive. We need our imagination to reason. Most importantly, in 1 Corinthians 13:1, Paul wrote, *"If I speak in the tongues of men or of angels, but do not have love, I am only a resounding gong or a clanging cymbal."* God's message transforms us and should always be given in love, for it is the loveliest message anyone will ever receive. We and our children need to understand why we believe and be able to convey it in words that draw others to Christ. Apologetics is the tool that we and our children can use to defend our biblical worldview.

WORLDVIEWS

To have a solid biblical worldview, you don't need to be well versed in the entirety of the Bible. You don't need to be a theologian to raise your children to follow Christ. As we grow closer to Christ and read the Word of God, His Holy Spirit transforms us so we can then share the gospel with others. It becomes our worldview!

One mother told me that her son once came home crying because one of his schoolmates told him, "God is not real." Instead of her son having full confidence in the reality of Jesus and the ability to stand strong in a loving manner to tell the other child that God is real, the boy came home in tears. The other boy had said that there was no way God could have made all the things in the world, adding, "I bet your mommy told you Santa Claus was real too, but he's not." Her son had recently learned that Santa was a myth, so he wondered if everything his mother had claimed about God was also a myth. That schoolmate's worldview did not reflect the one true God, and her son didn't know how to defend what he had known to be true.

When children are taught what to believe and the truth of those beliefs, they will be confident and prepared to defend them. This reinforces their *biblical worldview*, which helps to prevent them from being influenced by false doctrine. They are *"no longer…infants, tossed back and forth by the waves, and blown here and there by every wind of teaching and by the cunning and craftiness of people in their deceitful scheming"* (Ephesians 4:14). Help your child foster a desire to seek objective evidence in addition to personal testimony. Teach them how to recognize the voice of true authority that comes from you and God's Word.

Let's pray that the Lord will *engrave* His words on our children's minds and impress His directives into their hearts so these words become life to them. The word *engrave* means "to carve, score, imprint, and impress" as directed in the *Shema* in Deuteronomy 6.

Nature is the best way to help children see the evidence of God. Christian apologist Natasha Crain says there is a "cognitive science of religion…strong evidence that children are predisposed to interpret features of the natural world as having purpose— something called intuitive theism…born with a conceptual space for believing in a Creator or a Designer."[73]

Biblical knowledge and wisdom are needed to answer or defend the questions that the skeptical, secular world asks, either in seeking honest answers or in a desire to destroy truth. Most five-year-old children are not prepared to defend their faith. But just as they had to learn to walk before they could run, they must learn foundational biblical concepts that will help them uphold

---

73. Natasha Crain, *Talking with Your Kids about God: 30 Conversations Every Christian Parent Must Have* (Grand Rapids, MI: Baker Books, 2017), 119–120.

the Word of God. Teaching children about Jesus—who He is, what He has done, and how He loves them—is the starting point.

Let's prepare their hearts and minds so they will be able to defend what they believe and why. God's Word instructs us, *"Preach the word; be prepared in season and out of season; correct, rebuke and encourage—with great patience and careful instruction"* (2 Timothy 4:2).

How can we help our children to understand why a worldview based on God's promises is better than one based on man's? A biblical worldview answers four major questions:

+ Origin: *Where do I come from?*

+ Morality: *How do I determine good from evil?*

+ Purpose: *Why am I here? What is the meaning of life?*

+ Destiny: *What happens when I die?*

+ In addition, a viable worldview must have:

+ Logical consistency; consistently making perfect sense, being logically sound

+ Empirical adequacy; what it says about observable events are true

+ Experiential relevance; what we experience *actually* works in the world

Having a biblical worldview matters because we want our children to not only believe because they are told to do so, but because they know it is true and correct based on the fact that it is logical and works in their lives. We want them to have a Christian worldview that correctly answers where we come from and how we can determine morality logically. A worldview that answers these four questions and has these three factors is only the Christian worldview based upon the Word of God. Scripture becomes the basis on which we make all decisions!

IS THERE ABSOLUTE TRUTH?

Your child will soon face a world that believes there is no such thing as absolute truth, only your truth, my truth, and their truth. Help your child understand with absolute certainty that there is such a thing as absolute truth, contrary to the prevailing relativism. Here are a few excellent replies from the book *Tactics* by Gregory Koukl. One day, your child may hear such opinions as they become young adults in this ever-increasing evil world:

+ "There is no [such thing as] truth." (Is this a true statement?)

+ "There are no absolutes." (Is this an absolute?) [Or are you absolutely sure?]

+ "No one can know any truth about religion." (And how, precisely, did you come to know the truth about religion?)

+ "You can't know anything for sure." (Are you sure about that?)

+ "Talking about God is meaningless." (What does this statement about God mean?)

+ "You can only know truth through experience." (What experience taught you that truth?)

+ "Never take anyone's advice on that issue." (Should I take your advice on that?)[74]

Answering these skeptical statements with questions opens dialogue on both sides of the controversy and helps the other person think more profoundly. It has been claimed that Jesus

---

74. Gregory Koukl, *Tactics: A Game Plan for Discussing Your Christian Convictions* (Grand Rapids, MI: Zondervan 2009), 108.

answered more than three hundred questions with a question. You can use this technique with your child:

+ *Mommy, why do you read the Bible every day?* "Why do you think I read the Bible every day?"

+ *Daddy, what will be in heaven?* "What do you think will be in heaven?"

+ *Why do I have to be nice to my brother when he is mean to me?* "Why do you think you need to be nice to your brother when he's not being nice to you?"

The point is to equip your children to think about the answer before you answer them. When they answer something correctly, it builds up their confidence not only to ask questions but also to answer questions without the fear of being wrong. If they answer incorrectly, reassure them that their answer was understood and appreciated and then offer the correct answer. However, don't consistently make it a habit of answering every question with a question when they come seeking concrete information. This may exasperate your children and discourage their desire to ask questions.

APOLOGETIC Q&A FOR YOUNG CHILDREN

You should routinely have question-and-answer activities with your children. Use open-ended questions at times to get the conversation started and help you gauge what they are thinking about biblical truth. At other times, use a more direct approach, asking questions designed to help them know how to effectively communicate biblical truth to others. These activities can help you understand your child's comfort level in talking about what they believe. You can encourage them to exercise that spiritual muscle at home in order to be strong in the real world. Here are some questions you can use to start early:

+ *Who is God and who made God?*

God is the person who has made all the beautiful things we see—Mommy, Daddy, the sky, the plants, the animals, and you! No one made God. The word *God* means the one who has made all things and has always existed. It's kind of like when Mommy draws a pretty picture of a flower for you. The flower did not draw itself. Mommy had to draw it. We did not make ourselves, and the world did not make itself; God had to make everything. Some people don't understand what is real, and what is true. Maybe no one taught them. *(Refer to Genesis 1:1–31; Psalm 33:6; Colossians 1:16.)*

+ *What is God like?*

God is holy. *Holy* means He is perfect. He never does anything wrong or bad. God is sovereign. *Sovereign* means He is in control, and He is the boss of all things. Nothing happens without Him knowing or allowing it to happen. God is transcendent, which means He lives way up in heaven and is not physically with His creation. His Holy Spirit lives in our hearts. God hears all our prayers. God is omnipresent, which means God is always a part of our lives. He loves us, and His Holy Spirit is always with us. God is omnipotent, which means God is all-powerful. God can do anything He wants to do. Nothing can hold God back or stop Him. God is the real superhero! God is faithful, which means He will do whatever He says or promises. God is love. Just like I love you, and you love me, God loves us. God loved us first so we could love Him and others. *(Refer to Proverbs 19:21; Isaiah 57:15; Jeremiah 32:17; 1 Peter 1:16; Revelation 4:8.)*

+ *How do we know God made the earth?*

The Bible tells us that God made everything. The Bible tells the truth. The earth did not make itself. God is the only one who has the power to make us, all the animals, and this great, big earth. He made the earth in six days and rested on the seventh day. *(Refer to Genesis 1:1–31.)*

✦ *Why did God make the earth?*

God made the earth so we could have a wonderful place to live. He made the plants to feed us, and the sun to keep us warm. He made it perfect because He loves us. The earth is our home for the time we live here. One day, we will live in heaven, which is a perfect place. There will be no bad storms or anything that can make us afraid or sad. He made the earth so we can see His great love and power. *(Refer to Psalm 19:1; Hebrews 11:3.)*

✦ *Why did God make us?*

You know how Mommy and Daddy love you? Well, God loves you too. He made us because He loves us and wants us to be with Him forever in heaven. We are His family here on earth. God loves us more than anything, and that is why He made us. Besides feeling love for us, God can also feel sad, happy, or angry, just like we sometimes feel. God is love, and He made us to be just like Him, which is why we love each other. *(Refer to Genesis 1:26–27; Isaiah 43:7; Ephesians 2:10.)*

✦ *If God is love, and He loves us, why do bad things happen? Why am I sad sometimes?*

When God made the earth and the first people, Adam and Eve, everything was perfect. There was no sin, no bad things, and no sadness. Then the devil told them to do something God told them not to do. God said they could eat the fruit from any tree except from the tree that would bring death. They did not listen to God. They listened to the devil and ate from the tree that brought death into the world. Then everything changed. Sin came into the perfect world God had made. Sin is when you don't obey. Because Adam and

Eve disobeyed God, there is sin in the world, and bad things happen. *(Refer to Genesis 3:1–24; Romans 3:23.)*

✦ *What is sin, and how can Jesus take away my sin?*

When you sin, you also sin against God. God sent his Son Jesus to take away the sins of those who love God and His Son. God and Jesus love us so much that God allowed Jesus to die for our sins. We have to believe in Jesus and ask Him to save us from the penalty of our sins. *(Refer to Romans 6:23; 1 Peter 2:24.)*

✦ *What is hell, and why did God make hell if He loves us? (For younger children, you could use "a place of fire" if you do not want to use the word "hell.")*

Hell is a place full of fire. People who don't love God and His Son Jesus will live there forever. This is not what God wanted when He first made everything. He wanted all the people to love Him and live with Him. But some people refuse to love God and Jesus. God made heaven for us—a place where there will be no evil. It is a sin not to love and believe in God and His Son, Jesus. Remember that disobedience is sin. Disobedience is when you don't obey or listen. If you believe in Jesus, you will live in heaven with Him forever because Jesus took the punishment for our sins on the cross when He died. *(Refer to Matthew 25:46; 2 Thessalonians 1:8–9.)*

Sin, salvation, redemption, creation, heaven, and hell can be hard to explain to young children. Sometimes their questions and comments can be entertaining and comical. I remember reading about a girl who wanted to wear her bathing suit in the bathtub because she understood that God sees everything.

Most children are very inquisitive and will ask a plethora of questions. My son wanted to know how the dinosaurs fit into the ark, so I told him that a baby dinosaur was the size of a goat, making it easy for Noah to bring them. Would it surprise you to learn that a four-year-old asks as many as 200 to 300 questions a day?! That's why finding resources to guide them toward truth is advantageous.

Answers in Genesis (AiG)[75] in Petersburg, Kentucky, is an apologetics ministry that teaches the biblical story of a six-day creation and provides evidence for biblical truth. It highlights the purpose of understanding and teaching Genesis 1–11 and addresses many of the social issues we face today, including beliefs about creation, marriage, gender, and the foundation of sin, suffering, and atonement. Children are hearing false doctrine earlier than previous generations, and we need to be prepared to answer their questions with confidence and truth.

AiG also offers outstanding resources for children, including an Ark Encounter and Creation Museum.[76] The Ark Encounter is the largest timber frame structure in the world, containing three decks of world-class exhibits that answer questions about Noah's ark, Noah's family, the animals housed in the ark, and the flood. The Creation Museum, which is a forty-five-minute drive from the Ark Encounter, is exceptionally educational, with more than 140 state-of-the-art exhibits highlighting biblical creation and much more.

Another good resource is Summit Ministries,[77] which provides answers to some of the most challenging questions regarding Christianity and modern culture for ages sixteen to twenty-five. Based in Manitou Springs, Colorado, Summit is one of the most prominent organizations in training Christians in apologetics, social engagement, and worldview analysis. It helps the next generations understand God's truth so that they can develop a biblical worldview that they are confident in sharing with others. Summit's

---

75. answersingenesis.org/about.
76. answersingenesis.org/kids.
77. www.summit.org/about.

statements of faith and convictions focus on Christianity's essential doctrines to determine the correct behavior in society.

WHY IS THERE EVIL IF GOD IS SO GOOD?

I would guess that most people have contemplated this question. Children might ask, "Why do bad things happen?" or "Why do people do mean things?"

Common sense tells us if there is evil, then there must be good to gauge what is evil, and there must be a way to measure both. As Christians, we know that God's precepts and principles provide the measurements we need to determine right, wrong, good, and evil.

God did not create evil, which is the absence of good. God allowed evil to come into the world because man has free will to love God—or not. We are not forced to love God; instead, our love must be freely given to Him. God loved us first so we could love Him. He also allows evil for His purpose, which we come to understand when reading the book of Job.

One simple way to demonstrate evil and good to your children is to show a doughnut to them. Most of us love doughnuts and would say they are good, at least good to eat! The hole in the middle represents the absence of good. So evil is the absence of good.

SATAN WAITS TO ATTACK

Have you ever witnessed a cat on the prowl? He is crafty as he creeps slowly and quietly, only to attack at the perfect time to devour his prey. The devil is crafty too, roaming around like a lion that preys on the most vulnerable and young. (See 1 Peter 5:8.) He earnestly seeks to attack our children, and in Genesis 8:21, we read, *"Every inclination of the human heart is evil from childhood."* Double whammy!

Veteran researcher George Barna notes:

> And what easier way to inflict the maximum possible pain upon God than by winning over His beloved creatures from the earliest possible moment, resulting in a lifetime of unrighteous behavior by those creatures?...Satan knows well that if you destroy the character and hope of children, you rule the world![78]

The devil wants to train our children in the way he goes! He uses unctuous ways to draw children into his web of deception. Author Joy A. Schneider says, "Children are a threat to Satan, and he has no qualms about harming them. Their hearts and minds are canvases ready to receive their future painted upon them. The fight for the image on each child's canvas is the battle of the kingdoms."[79]

THE CHURCH MUST ENGAGE IN BATTLE

The whole body of Christ must be engaged and prepared to fight for our children. Imagine a church whose *priority* is to equip adults to effectively raise children to become outstanding warriors for Christ. Most church programs and sermons are directed toward adults, for adults. However, as the body of Christ, I feel we may be ignoring or neglecting one of our most vital parts: our children.

No one knows this better than Eileen, the children's director at a church I attended. Her passion for implementing truth and training in her ministry to the little ones was unsurpassed. Everyone at church praised the incredible job she was doing. But she knew more could be done to connect families through God's Word. She wanted to implement Sunday morning classes for

---

78. Barna, *Transforming Children into Spiritual Champions*, 50–51.
79. Joy A. Schneider, *How to Keep Grief from Stealing Your Destiny* (Fort Collins, CO: Water of Life Unlimited 2016), 129.

children, teens, and young adults that would follow the sermon series the pastor had planned for the adults. That way, moms and dads could go home and talk with their kids, whatever their ages, about how they felt and what they could do to implement what they had all learned at church the previous Sunday. Sadly, the budget committee did not see the value in restructuring the ministries.

God bless the children's ministry leaders who instill godly values and morals with little or no funding. More funds are allocated to missionary work than the mission to raise the next generation. A children's ministry budget will tell you how much they truly value the next generation.

There are divorce care programs, grief programs, youth groups, and marriage classes, all of which are vitally important. However, few programs, if any, guide adults on how to raise the next generation in Christ. Pastors need to take the lead role.

Theologian Joyce Ann Mercer says of pastors:

> They are not "above" involvement with the education of children. In fact, involvement with educating children is central to their pastoral ministry, as the bringing in of newcomers (children) to an identity and practice of Christian faith is the heart of the pastoral task of evangelism and mission.[80]

I am sure many parents would love to have the opportunity to attend a class at their church that would support them, walk beside them, guide them, and equip them to raise their children to become the next generation that will change the world to advance God's kingdom. With that understanding, there are many

---

80. Joyce Ann Mercer, *Welcoming Children: A Practical Theology of Childhood* (St. Louis, MO: Chalice Press, 2005), 206.

wonderful, godly, loving parents who are doing a great job raising the next generation, but I bet they wouldn't turn away any help!

Apologetics, if learned well and practiced often, can be an effective tool in our arsenal. It will also keep your child from the embarrassment of looking like a deer in the headlights when a secular professor, boss, neighbor, family member, or friend challenges their Christian beliefs. Paul admonishes us to:

> *Stand firm then, with the belt of truth buckled around your waist, with the breastplate of righteousness in place, and with your feet fitted with the readiness that comes from the gospel of peace.* (Ephesians 6:14–15)

Strap on that armor, get out the battle plan, recite the mission statement, and let's fight the war that has already been won in Christ!

11

INSTILLING VIRTUES IN CHILDREN

I remember the day my phone rang, and Travis's mother said, "I want to tell you what your son did today." I was taken aback...until I heard her say, "When the other boys said my son could not sit with them at their lunch table, your son said, 'He can sit here; he's my friend.' Your son is the first boy to make my son feel accepted. My son was crying happy tears in the car on the ride home." Later, when my son came home, I asked him what had happened. He told me he felt bad because the other boys were making fun of Travis for being overweight. My son did what he thought God would want him to do and welcomed Travis into their group. The other boys acquiesced because they liked my son.

At the teacher-parent conference, his teacher told me, "Every little boy wants to be his best friend, and every little girl wants to be his girlfriend. Your son is sweet and kind and funny too." My son was kind to everyone and is still a caring, virtuous person today. My daughter also has the same qualities. For example, she once asked a boy who had Tourette Syndrome to be her partner for a class project because she knew no one would choose him and she didn't want him to feel left out.

Having a virtuous character helps to make this sorry world a better place. Love is the greatest virtue of all. The word *virtue* means to behave in a way that exhibits high moral standards. It's the opposite of *vice*, which is moral depravity. Children naturally desire to fulfill their passions impulsively, so we need to teach them restraint and guide them to act and speak in a virtuous manner. This can be a difficult endeavor because their youthfulness can make children self-centered and self-serving.

Regarding virtue, Scripture tells us:

Make every effort to supplement your faith with virtue, and virtue with knowledge, and knowledge with self-control, and self-control with steadfastness, and steadfastness with godliness, and godliness with brotherly affection, and brotherly affection with love. For if these qualities are yours and are increasing, they keep you from being ineffective or unfruitful in the knowledge of our Lord Jesus Christ.

(2 Peter 1:5–8 esv)

Therefore, as God's chosen people, holy and dearly loved, clothe yourselves with compassion, kindness, humility, gentleness and patience. Bear with each other and forgive one another if any of you has a grievance against someone. Forgive as the Lord forgave you. And over all these virtues put on love, which binds them all together in perfect unity.

(Colossians 3:12–14)

Aristotle "believed that the function of a human was to engage in an activity of the soul in accordance with virtue [and] that there were two overriding virtues, intellectual and moral."[81]

The authors of *Growing Up Social* note:

---

81. Victoria Rayner, "12 Virtues Introduced by Aristotle – the master of those who know," *Aesthetic Healing Mindset*, June 12, 2011, aesthetichealingmindset. wordpress.com/2011/06/12/4706.

Kids know all sorts of things about video games, cartoons, and the latest apps. But they lack instruction about character. Virtues are behaviors that show high moral standards. Responsibility. Compassion. Persistence. Faith. There is no virtue app you can download into your child's heart and mind. Virtues are taught and caught as children observe and listen to their parents talk about what is right and what is wrong.[82]

Children need to have a relationship with the One who gave us His doctrine and theology. Remember, good theology gives rise to doxology, or praise to God. It is good to know *about* Jesus, but children also need to *know* Jesus, to *"taste and see that the LORD is good"* (Psalm 34:8), and to praise Him daily. Virtuous character helps our children draw closer to Jesus as they learn He is the most virtuous of all.

20 ESSENTIAL VIRTUES

Here are some virtues, Bible stories, and Bible verses that we should share with our children and model to the best of our ability. With the Word of God and much prayer, we can raise children who exhibit a virtuous, Christ-like character:

1. **Courage** — Not being fearful of the dark, bugs, or bullies. Learning how to be bold in faith at a young age will allow your children to freely share their faith as they get older, regardless of what others think. (See 1 Corinthians 16:13.) "Did you know that nowhere in the Bible are we ever instructed to ask for courage? We are always instructed to take courage...Deuteronomy

---

82. Gary Chapman and Arlene Pellicane, *Growing Up Social: Raising Relational Kids in a Screen-Driven World* (Chicago, IL: Northfield Publishing, 2014), 31.

31:6–12, 2 Chronicles 32:5–8, Daniel 10:17–19, Psalm 27:14, Psalm 31:24, Matthew 14:27, Mark 6:50…"[83]

Key Bible stories — Gideon Defeats the Midianites (Judges 7); David and Goliath (1 Samuel 17); Jesus in the garden of Gethsemane (Matthew 26:39)

Bible verses — Mark 6:50; Acts 4:13

2. **Temperance** — Having self-control and restraint, not biting, hitting, or falling into peer pressure. Learning this early will help children avoid the sinful desires of the flesh when great restraint and self-control are needed. (See Galatians 5:16.) It's easy for children to act out because they want what others have, but it's our job as parents to help them understand that self-control will also protect them against projected evil in the world.

   Bible stories — David spares Saul's life (1 Samuel 24:1–14)

   Bible verses — Galatians 5:22–24; 2 Peter 1:5–6

3. **Honor** — To be respectful to others, especially to parents, teachers, and elders. Honor those who are in charge and have authority over you. Act honorably in all situations. (See Hebrews 13:18.) Learning how to have honor and respect for authority early in life can help our children avoid behaviors that lead to expulsion from school or time in jail. Honor supersedes a sense of "I have a right to this" and allows one to put others before self.

   Bible stories — Mary praises God (Luke 1:46–55); Jesus washes His disciples' feet (John 13:1–17).

---

83. Kevin White, *Audacious Generosity: How to Experience, Receive, and Give More Than You Ever Thought Possible* (Carol Stream, IL: Tyndale House Publishers, 2020), 83.

Bible verses — John 5:23; Romans 12:10; 1 Peter 2:17

4. **Good Temper** — Not allowing uncontrolled anger such as tantrums or outbursts to be an acceptable form of behavior. Try to anticipate what may be a pattern that triggers a tantrum and prepare for it ahead of time. Remember to empathize with their feelings. Make sure they know you understand what they are feeling and know that you love them. Be wise and address anger right from the start. (See Proverbs 29:11). A tempestuous personality will cause much pain and heartache for both child and parent. Pastor and counselor Reb Bradley says, "Distracting may be a quick way to settle down a distraught or angry child, but it cannot be a substitute for discipline that will subdue the will."[84] Dr. Scott Turansky also offers excellent resources for disciplining at BiblicalParenting.org.

Bible stories — Cain and Abel (Genesis 4:2–12); Moses flees to Midian (Exodus 2:11–14)

Bible verses — Proverbs 15:1; James 1:19

5. **Friendliness** — Being kind, even when they do not feel like being kind. Friendliness is a form of grace that your child offers you, another child, or any other person in their lives. The more they practice being a good friend to others, the more they will learn that a good friend looks out for others regardless of how others treat them. (See Luke 6:31.) When they learn to be friendly, they will be able to choose good friends and become great team players in sports, school, church, and life.

Bible story — A friend comes at midnight (Luke 11:5–8)

---

84. Bradley, *Child Training Tips*, 67.

Bible verses — Proverbs 17:17; John 15:13–15; 1 Corinthians 15:33

6. **Truthfulness** — Being honest at all times. Always discipline for lying, so they can present themselves as being truthful, never being ashamed. (See 2 Timothy 2:15.) Those who are caught in lies feel the consequences of shame. One little lie can turn into two little lies, and before you know it, your child has become a compulsive liar. Set a good example by not lying yourself. You don't want to tell your child to answer the phone and tell the caller you are not there. These little white lies and exaggerations are not acceptable. Trial lawyer Gerry Spence notes, "Truth-telling has been designated as the highest of virtues in every culture."[85] However, it's possible to lie for noble reasons, as was the case when Rahab protected two Hebrew spies and the midwives refused to kill baby boys. (See, respectively, Joshua 2:4–7; Exodus 1:15–22.)

   Bible story — Ananias and Sapphira (Acts 5:1–11)

   Bible verses — Psalm 15:2; Ephesians 4:25

7. **Justice** — Being fair and expecting fairness comes with understanding that sometimes things in life are not fair, and your child does not have to seek remedy or retribution for unjust deeds. (See Hebrews 10:30.) Children need to learn that God is just even when His actions don't seem to be fair. For example, in the parable about the workers in the field, everyone was justly paid a full day's wage although some did not work the full day. God is just to all and can be gracious in His generosity if He chooses to do so.

---

85. Gerry Spence, *How to Argue and Win Every Time* (New York: St. Martin's Press, 1995), 54.

Bible stories — The parable of the workers in the vineyard (Matthew 20:1–16); the parable of the persistent widow (Luke 18:1–8)

Bible verses — Isaiah 1:17; Luke 18:7

8. **Charity** — Always be willing to share and give to others. Explain that what your children do for others, they are really doing for Jesus. (See Proverbs 19:17.) Jesus said it is better to give than to receive. (See Acts 20:35.) You want your children to be able to say, "It brings me greater joy in my heart to give to others than when others give to me," which takes practice. Charity also affords your children the opportunity to understand that the needs of others are most important. Winston Churchill once said, "You make a living at what you get, and you make a life out of what you give." We need to show our children that giving always pays off.

Bible stories — Moses and the Israelites construct the sanctuary (Exodus 36:1–7); the collection for the Lord's people (2 Corinthians 8:1–15)

Bible verses — 2 Corinthians 9:6–8; 1 John 3:17

9. **Discipline** — Allowing your children to feel in control when things seem out of control. Self-discipline will help them to have the power to turn away from evil enticements and traps set by the devil (see 2 Timothy 1:7) and keep them safe from harm as well. Discipline requires that you help them set up a structure to begin their own disciplines in the areas of their lives that mean the most. We need to be hands-on to help our children understand and apply discipline. Keeping a chart or having family meetings is a good way to implement discipline.

Bible story — Jesus is tested in the wilderness (Luke 4:1–13)

Bible verses — Proverbs 25:28; 29:11

10. **Purity** — Learning to respect their mind and body and seek what is pure and good. This will allow children to turn away from things that are sinful later in life. (See 1 Timothy 5:22.) Purity is more of a lifestyle than a word you teach. Purity is a gift they can give to their future spouse. Staying pure can keep them safe from becoming indecent, depraved, immodest, sick, and defiled. Dress your child modestly; it is a shame how some parents dress their children to look *sexy*.

Bible story — John the Baptist (Matthew 3)

Bible verses — Proverbs 20:11; Matthew 5:8; Philippians 4:8

11. **Wisdom** — Instilling a desire for knowledge and praying to Jesus for wisdom to know what is true. (See Proverbs 1:7.) A child's worldview should be anchored in biblical truth. The definition of the word *true* can only include the character of God. Help your children to give their will to God. Theologian Norman L. Geisler wrote, "Being willing is essential. Evidence cannot convince the unwilling."[86] Pastor Erwin W. Lutzer notes, "Your will is your decision-making faculty. Often it is caught between your thoughts and your desires. Your emotions express how you feel, your mind says what you know, but your will decides the direction you will go."[87] Believers walk in wisdom using godly knowledge and

---

86. Norman L. Geisler and Frank Turek, *I Don't Have Enough Faith to Be an Atheist* (Wheaton, IL: Crossway, 2004), 44.
87. Lutzer, *How to Break a Stubborn Habit*, 115.

understanding. Your children can learn this as you help them apply wisdom to daily decisions.

Bible stories — Solomon's prayer for wisdom (1 Kings 3:5–15); the wise and foolish builders (Matthew 7:24–27)

Bible verses — Proverbs 2:6; James 1:5; 3:17

12. **Forbearance** — Learning to have restraint under provocation or upsetting speech. Not hitting back, not exchanging hurtful words. Letting the sin of another go without retribution. (See Romans 3:25; Colossians 3:13.) Having patience during suffering. Forbearance is a tool to protect your children's feelings against bullies. Equip them to respond in a nonthreatening way when others want to stir up dissension. This can be accomplished through role play.

Bible story — David spares Saul's life (1 Samuel 24)

Bible verses — Matthew 5:38–41; Ephesians 4:2

13. **Empathy and Compassion** — Identifying, imagining, and showing understanding for how others feel in various situations, feeling or understanding their pain. (See Matthew 22:39.) Even babies exhibit these traits early on; they usually start to cry when they hear another baby cry. (See Romans 12:15.) Sympathy, on the other hand, means that you pity the other person or feel sorry for the situation, which you see from *your* point of view instead of finding out how the person is feeling.

Bible story — The parable of the Good Samaritan (Luke 10:25–37)

Bible verses — Matthew 14:14; Luke 6:27–31; Colossians 3:12

14. **Perseverance/Persistence** — Not giving up on the first, second, or third try. If it is worthy and good, it is worth the work. Encourage your children not to give up. Perseverance and persistence will help them when they face challenging obstacles in the future, such as difficulties in their job or marriage. *"The plans of the diligent lead to profit"* (Proverbs 21:5). Help them to be diligent and take initiative in their desire to learn. David A. R. White, an actor, producer, and author, notes, "Everyone is going to fail from time to time, but you are only considered a 'failure' when you allow failure to defeat you. You are only a failure when you give up and refuse to try again. Remember, there is a difference between failing and being a failure."[88]

    Bible stories — Wickedness in the world (Genesis 6–7); the parable of the persistent widow (Luke 18:1–8)

    Bible verses — Matthew 24:13; 2 Thessalonians 1:4; James 1:4

15. **Respect** — Learning to be respectful at all times, even with those who are not respectful toward you. *"Do not repay evil with evil"* (1 Peter 3:9). Respect and honor go hand in hand. Learning to be respectful can one day save an important relationship. It is paramount that children learn to say "please" and "thank you." Otherwise, they will have the impression that the world revolves around them, and they can get what they want without expressing their gratitude. Having a selfish attitude may cause a child to become thoughtless toward the rights and feelings of others. Likewise, they should always reply, "You're welcome" after someone has thanked them. Encourage your children to send handwritten thank-you notes too.

---

88. David A. R. White, *Between Heaven and Hollywood: Chasing Your God-Given Dream* (Grand Rapids, MI: Zondervan, 2016), 90.

> *Bible stories* — Artaxerxes sends Nehemiah to Jerusalem (Nehemiah 2:1–8); Jesus respected Mary and Joseph (Luke 2:51); God tells us to respect authority (Romans 13:1–7).
>
> *Bible verses* — Ephesians 6:1–3; 1 Peter 2:17

16. **Faith** — Learning to have faith in our Lord Jesus will allow your children to be strong when they feel weak or find themselves dealing with a mean person. Faithfulness will bring blessings. (See Proverbs 28:20.) They need to understand that faith comes from listening, obeying, and believing. There is a difference between hearing and listening. We can involuntarily hear, but we actively listen for comprehension and action. Hearing is through the ears but listening transforms the heart and mind. At night, ask your child if they believe the sun will rise in the morning, bringing a new day. That is an example of faith.

    Bible stories — Abraham tested (Genesis 22); David and Goliath (1 Samuel 17)

    Bible verses — Romans 10:17; 2 Corinthians 5:7

17. **Mercy and Forgiveness** — Extending forgiveness to someone who has hurt you is an expression of mercy. Forgiveness takes the power away from the offender and gives the person who was wronged freedom from anger and hurt. Instruct your children to be merciful like Jesus. (See Luke 6:36.) However, balance mercy with justice and acknowledge the pain your child feels. It may take time for them to forgive an offender. We are commanded to forgive others their trespasses against us and forgive them many times. (See Matthew 6:12; 18:21–22.) What an amazing world we would have if we could all learn to truly forgive others continually and

unconditionally. The goal of forgiveness is reconciliation with each other and Christ.

Bible stories — The parable of the unmerciful servant (Matthew 18:21–35)

Bible verses — Matthew 9:13; Ephesians 2:4–5

18. **Thankfulness and Gratitude** — The quality of being appreciative for what you have or toward other people's kind actions. Children can learn how to be thankful in all situations, which will help them to experience the world and relationships in a positive manner. *"Give thanks in all circumstances; for this is God's will for you in Christ Jesus"* (1 Thessalonians 5:18). Children learn by example, and they need to witness the adults in their lives saying thank you and expressing gratitude, even for small gestures. Children recognize gratitude in behavior, words, and facial expressions. Gratitude brings people closer together in appreciation and love.

Bible stories — Jesus heals ten men with leprosy (Luke 17:11–19)

Bible verses — Psalm 105:1; Ephesians 5:20; Philippians 4:6

19. **Prayerfulness** — One of the most important virtues. Children should learn how to pray to the Lord naturally, like talking to family members. Pray with your children and let them see and hear you praying to the Lord. Prayer is an act of obedience and brings peace to one's soul. (See Philippians 4:6.) Prayer is the only way we can converse with God.

Bible stories — The Lord's Prayer (Matthew 6:9–13); the parable of the persistent widow (Luke 18:1–8); Jesus prays to be glorified (John 17:1–5)

Bible verses — Jeremiah 29:12; Colossians 4:2; 1 Thessalonians 5:16–18

20. **Humility** — Willing to be a servant to others instead of thinking they should be serving you. Dr. Kathy Koch says, "Serving motivates children to develop character and skills...builds overall confidence, decreases self-centeredness, develops compassion for others, and can lay a lifetime foundation where giving to others is second nature."[89] If children want to make friends, they need to exhibit a humble attitude. Rick Warren once said, "True humility is not thinking less of yourself; it is thinking of yourself less."

Bible stories — A warning against hypocrisy (Matthew 23:1–38); John testifies again about Jesus (John 3:22–36)

Bible verses — Numbers 12:3; Philippians 2:8; James 4:6

VIRTUE STONES

Pairing virtues with stones can be an effective and fun teaching tool. Scripture tells us that the foundations of the city walls of the New Jerusalem are *"decorated with every kind of precious stone"* (Revelation 21:19). In his book *Heaven*, Randy Alcorn says, "The precious stones and gold represent incredible wealth, suggestive of the exorbitant riches of God's splendor."[90] Revelation 21:21 says, *"The twelve gates were twelve pearls, each gate made of a single pearl. The great street of the city was of gold, as pure as transparent glass."* We are also compared to *"living stones...being built into a spiritual house to be a holy priesthood, offering spiritual sacrifices acceptable to God through Jesus Christ"* (1 Peter 2:5).

Take twelve white stones and paint them different colors so that each one represents one of the virtues. Use them to discuss

89. Koch, *Start with the Heart*, 99.
90. Randy Alcorn, *Heaven* (Chicago, IL: Tyndale House Publishers, 2004), 248.

what it means to have self-control, love, truthfulness, forgiveness, or any of the other virtues. Print out a picture of the real stone, glue it onto an index card, and then write the name and description of the virtue. Give examples according to what your children can comprehend and understand.

As you use the virtue stones with your children, make sure to explain that the stones do not have magical powers; they are only symbols to help us remember good virtues.

1. **Jasper** (red, yellow, brown quartz) — comfort and security (courage, justice)

2. **Sapphire** (blue) — stone of wisdom, bringing insight (wisdom, persistence)

3. **Chalcedony** (translucent milky/gray crystal) — benevolence and generosity (charity, discipline)

4. **Emerald Sardonyx** (green) — symbol of rebirth (honor)

5. **Sardonyx** (onyx/black) — self-control (temperance, honor, good temper, forbearance, moderation)

6. **Ruby** (red) — good fortune, pure love, and loyalty (friendliness, purity)

7. **Chrysolite** (yellowish-green sapphire) — self-esteem (humility)

8. **Beryl** (aquamarine) — protection and communication (truthfulness)

9. **Topaz** (brownish yellow crystal) — truth and forgiveness (empathy, mercy)

10. **Chrysoprase** (aquamarine gemstone) — love and prosperity (respect)

11. **Jacinth** (orange red variety of zircon) — protection (prudence)

12. **Amethyst** (purple quartz) — wisdom and understanding (faith)

Have fun with the stones. For example, give your children a stone for the day, making sure they understand that the stones have no power but are symbols to remember various virtues. If you give them topaz, ask them to make sure to tell the truth and remember to forgive someone. Praise them for doing so and then give them another stone the next day to practice another virtue.

These are moments that make learning fun and engaging, which will help your child to remember the virtue you are trying to instill.

Jesus is our Rock, our cornerstone, and our sure foundation. Here are some verses you can share with your children as you talk about the rocks they hold in their hands as a symbol of Christ:

+ Psalm 61:2–3 — *"From the ends of the earth I call to you, I call as my heart grows faint; lead me to the **rock** that is higher than I. For you have been my refuge, a strong tower against the foe."*

+ Psalm 62:2 — *"Truly he is my **rock** and my salvation; he is my fortress, I will never be shaken."*

+ Psalm 118:22–23 — *"The **stone** the builders rejected has become the **cornerstone**; the Lord has done this, and it is marvelous in our eyes."*

+ Isaiah 8:14 — *"He will be a holy place; for both Israel and Judah he will be a **stone** that causes people to stumble and a **rock** that makes them fall."*

+ Isaiah 26:4 — *"Trust in the Lord forever, for the Lord, the Lord himself, is the **Rock** eternal."*

+ Isaiah 28:16 — *"So this is what the Sovereign Lord says: 'See, I lay a **stone** in Zion, a tested **stone**, a precious **cornerstone** for* *a sure foundation; the one who relies on it will never be stricken with panic.'"*

+ Isaiah 44:8 — *"You are my witnesses. Is there any God besides me? No, there is no other **Rock**; I know not one."*

+ Daniel 2:34–35 — *"While you were watching, a **rock** was cut out, but not by human hands. It struck the statue on its feet of iron and clay and smashed them…the **rock** that struck the statue became a huge mountain and filled the whole earth."*

+ Zechariah 10:4 — *"From Judah will come the **cornerstone**, from him the tent peg, from him the battle bow, from him every ruler."*

+ Matthew 7:24 — *"Therefore everyone who hears these words of mine and puts them into practice is like a wise man who built his house on the **rock**."*

+ Matthew 21:42–44 — *"Have you never read in the Scriptures: 'The **stone** the builders rejected has become the **cornerstone**; the Lord has done this, and it is marvelous in our eyes'? Therefore I tell you that the kingdom of God will be taken away from you and given to a people who will produce its fruit. Anyone who falls on this **stone** will be broken to pieces; anyone on whom it falls will be crushed."*

+ First Corinthians 3:11 — *"For no one can lay any **foundation** other than the one already laid, which is Jesus Christ."*

+ Ephesians 2:19–22 — *"Consequently, you are no longer foreigners and strangers, but fellow citizens with God's people and also members of his household, built on the **foundation** of the apostles and prophets, with Christ Jesus himself as the chief **cornerstone**. In him the whole building is joined together and rises to become a holy temple in the Lord. And in him you too are being built together to become a dwelling in which God lives by his Spirit."*

In Exodus 28:18 (ESV), the second row on the priestly garment includes a diamond. A diamond is a gemstone that declares, "I love you." A symbol of everlasting love, it's the hardest substance known on earth, it will not react under intense heat, and it's the most valuable of all gemstones. I don't know about you, but when I think about a diamond, I think about Jesus!

May these fascinating finds about stones and Scripture verses about Jesus give you new ways to connect with your children as you instill virtues that will help them to be more like our Savior.

12

INSTILLING FRUIT OF THE SPIRIT

I pray this chapter will help your child understand each fruit of the Holy Spirit and its purpose in God's economy.

Children are the fruit of the womb, a great reward and a great blessing. We are commanded to raise them up in the Lord so the fruit of the Spirit can dwell deeply within them and be seen in their actions and deeds. God's Word tells us:

> But the fruit of the Spirit is love, joy, peace, forbearance, kindness, goodness, faithfulness, gentleness and self-control. Against such things there is no law. (Galatians 5:22–23)

The best way to teach your children the concepts of the fruit of the Spirit is to explain what each one means and show them by example through your words and actions.

Fruit trees bear fruit during a specific season. After producing delicious fruit for us to eat, the tree will not produce any more fruit until the next season. However, every person who reads God's Word and obeys it is like a tree that always produces fruit, no matter what the season. Fully grasping the concept of each fruit of the Spirit will help you to educate your children.

Matthew Sleeth, executive director of Blessed Earth, points out:

> Christianity is the only religion that weaves trees from one end of its sacred text to the other. Every important character and every major event has a tree marking the spot.[91]

LOVE

> *For God so loved the world that he gave his one and only Son, that whoever believes in him shall not perish but have eternal life.* (John 3:16)

> *"Love the Lord your God with all your heart and with all your soul and with all your mind and with all your strength...Love your neighbor as yourself." There is no commandment greater than these.* (Mark 12:30–31)

The Greek word for *love* in these Bible verses is *agape*. Agape love is perfect love that puts others first, before self, in thought and action. It's the highest form of love, the love God has for His creation. *"God is love"* (1 John 4:8), and Jesus demonstrates His love with His words and deeds. Love is many wonderful things, but mostly, love is compassionate, considerate, giving, and selfless. Throughout the New Testament, we learn of the Father and the Son's love for each other. (See, for example, Matthew 3:17; John 14:31.)

Love includes other fruit as well. *"Love is patient, love is kind"* (1 Corinthians 13:4). Love is a choice. God commands us to love

---

91. Matthew Sleeth, MD, *Reforesting Faith: What Trees Teach Us About the Nature of God and His Love for Us* (New York: WaterBrook, 2019), 5.

each other because *"love covers over a multitude of sins"* (1 Peter 4:8).

Love can best be taught through words and actions. Make sure to tell your children often that you love them and why you love them. Use words of affirmation. Your love can be shown in action through hugs and kisses as well as taking care of their needs, wants, and desires.

JOY

For what is our hope, our joy, or the crown in which we will glory in the presence of our Lord Jesus when he comes? Is it not you? (1 Thessalonians 2:19)

Joy is expressed in happiness. In his book *Happiness*, Randy Alcorn notes, "Children laugh an average of four hundred times daily, adults only fifteen."[92]

Blaise Pascal said that all people, without exception, seek happiness; Thomas Aquinas expressed that people crave spiritual joy; Augustine claimed that every person desires to be happy; and Ignatius wished for an "abundance of happiness." Randy Alcorn looked for references to *joy* in the Word of God. He says, "I've studied more than 2,700 scripture passages where words such as *joy, happiness, gladness, merriment, pleasure, celebration, cheer, laughter, delight, jubilation, feasting, exultation and celebration* are used."[93]

Happiness is a quality that helps us in every area of our lives, including family, community, friendships, and careers. GoodThink founder Shawn Achor notes, "Data abounds showing that happy workers have higher levels of productivity, produce higher sales, perform better in leadership positions, and receive

92. Randy Alcorn, *Happiness* (Carol Stream, IL: Tyndale House Publishers, 2015), 4.
93. Ibid., 19.

higher performance ratings and higher pay...happiness *causes* success and achievement."[94]

In one experiment, four-year-old children who were told to think about something happy before they were instructed to complete a task outperformed other children who were not told to think happy thoughts before they started.[95] God's Word tells us, *"Rejoice always, pray continually, give thanks in all circumstances; for this is God's will for you in Christ Jesus"* (1 Thessalonians 5:16–18). Help your child learn to be joyful in all situations.

PEACE

> *For to us a child is born, to us a son is given, and the government will be on his shoulders. And he will be called Wonderful Counselor, Mighty God, Everlasting Father, Prince of Peace.*
>
> (Isaiah 9:6)

Jesus gives us His peace for He says, *"Peace I leave with you; my peace I give you"* (John 14:27). We are called to be peacemakers, not just peacekeepers. (See Matthew 5:9.) The late theology professor James Innell Packer said, *"Peace* here means an end to hostility, guilt, and exposure to the retributive punishment that was otherwise unavoidable—in other words, pardon for all the past and permanent personal acceptance for the future."[96]

It is the duty of Christians to seek peace with others and within ourselves. Help your children learn to enjoy quiet time early in life. This is a great tool for them to use when they become upset and don't know how to get control of their big emotions.

---

94. Shawn Achor, *The Happiness Advantage: How a Positive Brain Fuels Success in Work and Life* (New York: Crown Currency, 2010), 41–42.
95. Ibid., 46.
96. J. I. Packer, *Concise Theology: A Guide to Historic Christian Beliefs* (Wheaton, IL: Tyndale House, 1993), 132.

When they close their eyes and breathe deeply, they will be able to defuse anger when they feel it starting to brew up from within. A simple technique that will become second nature to them is to have them call upon the Lord with a short sentence such as, "Jesus loves me," or "Jesus, help me to be calm."

PATIENCE

I was shown mercy so that in me, the worst of sinners, Christ Jesus might display his immense patience as an example for those who would believe in him and receive eternal life.

(1 Timothy 1:16)

We are wise to be patient doers of the Word as we wait for our Lord's return. Patience is connected with other fruit as well. (See, for example, Romans 12:12; Ephesians 4:2; Colossians 3:12.) The book of Job provides us with an exceptional example of patience while enduring suffering.

It is hard for young children to be patient while waiting their turn; they often fight against the idea of putting others first. Teaching them to love others can help them learn to be patient. They need to understand that *they* are not the center of the world; *Jesus* is! Early on, children need to learn that fulfillment of desires may take time. Learning to be patient will help your child avoid becoming a rude, vitriolic, self-serving, self-centered adult.

KINDNESS

But when the kindness and love of God our Savior appeared, he saved us, not because of righteous things we had done, but because of his mercy. He saved us through the washing of rebirth and renewal by the Holy Spirit. (Titus 3:4–5)

Jesus reaches out His loving hand for us to grasp, demonstrating kindness in all He did while on this earth and all He still does for us by forgiving our sins and interceding for us with the Father. In 1889, John Chrysostum wrote:

> He takes away "anger," he puts in "kindness;" he takes away "bitterness," he puts in "tender-heartedness;" he extirpates "malice" and "railing," he plants "forgiveness" in their stead.[97]

Being respectful is an act of kindness toward others. Help your child learn to respect the law and other people's property, personal space, and feelings. Instruct them to use words that are respectful and not hurtful.

GOODNESS

Give thanks to the LORD, *for he is good; his love endures forever.*   (Psalm 118:1)

Jesus is the epitome of all that is good. Everything He has done and will do is for our well-being. God gives us all we need and want according to *"his good, pleasing and perfect will"* (Romans 12:2). The Greek word for *goodness* means "uprightness of heart and life." More than a moral behavior, goodness is an excellent character trait.

One synonym for the word *goodness* is *grace*. Explain to your child that God's grace is a perfect example of goodness. When your child is very young, it's best not to ask them to *be good* because

---

97. Saint Chrysostom, "Homilies on Ephesians, XVI," ed. Dr. Philip Schaff, *Saint Chrysostom: Homilies on Galatians, Ephesians, Philippians, Colossians, Thessalonians, Timothy, Titus, and Philemon,* vol. 13 (New York: Charles Scribner's Sons, 1905), 127.

that's an abstract concept for them. Clinical psychologist Laura Markham notes that a toddler "can't yet control most of his behavior, and he can't really distinguish between his emotions (his 'self') and his behavior, so even if you're careful to say, 'It's bad to hit,' instead of 'You're a bad boy!' the distinction is lost on him."[98]

As your children mature, you can explain the type of behavior you expect of them. When they behave properly, you can say "good job." They will eventually connect the action with the term and will understand what it means to *be good*.

FAITHFULNESS

But the Lord is faithful, and he will strengthen you and protect you from the evil one.   (2 Thessalonians 3:3)

Jesus will never leave nor forsake us, and His honesty is always faithful and true. He gives us faith so that we will believe in Him.

Children learn about being faithful from the actions of others toward them. They learn faith in action when they are sure that you will always feed them, love them, and provide for them. Ask your children if they think that Mommy and Daddy will always take care of them. When they reply *yes*, tell them that is what faithfulness means. "*Faith is the substance of things hoped for, the evidence of things not seen*" (Hebrews 11:1 NKJV).

GENTLENESS

Take my yoke upon you and learn from me, for I am gentle and humble in heart, and you will find rest for your souls.
                                                    (Matthew 11:29)

---

98. Dr. Laura Markham, *Peaceful Parent, Happy Kids: How to Stop Yelling and Start Connecting* (New York: Penguin Group, 2012), 102.

Jesus is strong enough to hold the world in His hands and gentle enough to comfort and protect us under His wings.

Children can learn how to be gentle by giving them a small pet to love and take care of. My children were very gentle when handling and speaking to our puppy, Princess. She was so small and fragile. Now that they are adults, they hold a special love for all of God's creatures.

God, the greatest power in the universe, has a gentle love for us and yet it's all powerful. Explain to your child about how powerful the wind is in a storm and yet how gentle it can be as it blows lightly across their face. God is both powerful and gentle.

SELF-CONTROL

Do you not know that your bodies are temples of the Holy Spirit, who is in you, whom you have received from God? You are not your own; you were bought at a price. Therefore honor God with your bodies. (1 Corinthians 6:19–20)

Jesus is in control of all things, including His sacrifice on the cross. He demonstrated His power in self-control when He allowed Himself to be beaten and crucified. He was obedient unto death.

Learning self-control can prevent a child from becoming a compulsive drinker, gambler, or liar, for example, later in life. Those who practice self-control have better health and better relationships. To help children learn how to have self-control, you will have to guide them and give them opportunities to practice self-control.

13

HAVE FUN LEARNING TOGETHER

When my husband Guy was ten, he received a tool set for Christmas. He was so happy to get a hammer, screwdriver, and ruler, but his favorite tool was his little saw. This was a time when toy manufacturing regulations were not as strict, and these were real working tools for little hands. The day after Christmas, his mother was shocked to discover that Guy had sawed one of the couch boards in half!

At any age, it's important to learn how to use tools correctly. I believe the greatest combination of tools to build a strong foundation in God and His Son Jesus are godly, intentional parenting and the Word of God. Being intentional means thinking ahead about the moral development and character traits we want to instill in our children and how we will work daily to achieve that. It's not about doing more; God knows parents have a lot on their plate. It's about being effective and intentional in what we do while relying on the guidance of the Holy Spirit to transform us and our children.

FAMILY MISSION STATEMENT

Besides planning, setting goals, and using tools, you can write a family mission statement—a covenant with the Lord. A mission statement will clearly delineate your family's goals to serve and honor the Lord, raise each child to love Him, and effectively educate them in Christian values and Christian doctrine. After you write a mission statement, have the whole family read it together daily. Every January, sit down as a family to read it, talk about it, and evaluate how you are living up to it or not. Make changes for the coming year, much like establishing some New Year's resolutions.

Not sure how to get started? Use this example of a family mission statement to help:

By the grace of our Lord and Savior, we will diligently:

Love the Lord Jesus Christ with all our hearts, minds, souls, and strengths, day by day and moment by moment.

Praise Him and give thanks to Him daily and attend church faithfully.

Submit to God's authority in every area of our lives.

Joyfully spread the gospel message.

Pray morning, noon, and night, asking the Holy Spirit to fill us and guide us.

Exhibit our faith in words and deeds inside and outside of the home.

Raise our children in the ways of the Lord and make sure they learn solid biblical doctrine.

Be respectful, honest, and loving always.

As a family, seek to love and help others and be self-sacrificial in honor of the Father, Son, and His Holy Spirit. Amen.

This is a lifelong mission but, more importantly, it is an honor and privilege. After all, God's Word says only a few will be blessed to enter the kingdom of heaven. (See Matthew 7:13–14.)

16 FUN WAYS TO PREPARE THE SOIL

Every little action done daily will help to create rich soil to enable godly seeds to grow deep roots, building that foundation in Christ. I hope and pray that the following ideas will help you to raise your children in a way that places Jesus in the prominent place of their hearts and minds. Some of these can be tweaked for older children:

+ **When babies look into a mirror and smile:** Say, "Jesus loves you!" You are connecting those happy emotions with the name of Jesus.

+ **When you show them God's creation:** Say, "Jesus is bright like the sun," "Jesus is beautiful like the moon," or "Jesus is strong like the trees." Children love metaphors and similes. Jesus uses metaphors to help us understand that He is the door, a vine, and bread.

+ **Destiny land, not Disneyland:** Decorate your children's bedrooms with biblical characters that they can relate to and emulate. Children have keen observational abilities and vivid imaginations; they will act out the behaviors of the characters they are familiar with.

+ **Moments in time:** When you notice your toddler looking to see if you are watching them, say, "I'm here, and Jesus is here, too," or, "I see you, and Jesus sees you, too." Because He is there!

+ **Feeding:** For infants, toddlers, and young children, at every meal, even at snack time, say, "Thank You, Jesus, for our food." Nursing infants should hear His name and connect their needs being met with the name of Jesus. Say, "Jesus loves you!" Remember, we are preparing the soil at this age.

+ **Placemats:** Make homemade placemats. Have your child draw pictures of Jesus, God, the Bible, or cut out biblical pictures from magazines and have them laminated to use as placemats. Write Bible verses. Once they learn the message, make a new one. This is a great tool for memorizing Bible verses for all ages.

+ **Nap time:** Instead of saying, "Let's take a nap," say, "Let's take a Sabbath's rest (or Sabbath's nap) and say a prayer to Jesus." You are creating a category and vocabulary in their mind. Later, you can explain the full meaning of a Sabbath's rest. You are planting seeds into rich soil to grow deep roots. Resting in Jesus is a posture of trust that God will take care of all things.

+ **Give them a turn as a church leader:** Have them read from their Bible and preach to the family. Let them "baptize" their doll in the bathtub or pool. Instead of always playing tea party, let them give bread and juice for communion to family members.

+ **Make a prayer calendar:** Take a large piece of cardboard and have your child put stickers or draw what they will pray for each day of the week. You can also use a whiteboard or a felt board so it can be reused. On Saturday, have them choose what the family will pray about each day for the next week.

+ **Look, See, and Tell:** Take a large glass jar and fill it with sand or rice. Place biblical trinkets that represent a specific holiday and biblical characters inside. Make sure the lid is taped shut so they cannot open it. They can "look, see, and tell" the things they find as they turn the jar. Ask them to explain what they found and how it relates to that specific holiday or Bible story.

+ **A journal for Jesus:** Have your child color or draw in their journal everything they learned about Jesus. As they get older, have them write a few words; before you know it, they will write sentences. It will be fun for them to look back and see how their skills improved as their faith grew.

+ **Monthly gift box:** Spend one-on-one time with your child because that is the perfect gift! Label twelve envelopes for each month. In each envelope, place surprises, such as tickets to a movie, bowling, laser tag, picnic, swimming, horseback riding, and other activities. Include a biblical theme or story for that event. For example, the story of Jesus feeding the multitude with the picnic lunch, the story of the battle of Jericho with laser tag, or Moses crossing the Red Sea with swimming.

+ **Paddle game:** Make two *paddle faces*, one happy and one sad, using a ruler and cardstock. Play a game of *Happy or Sad*, asking them, "Would Jesus like it if you told a lie?" or "Would Jesus like it if you shared your toy?" Have them hold up the paddle they think is the correct answer and ask them why they chose that one. Then praise them for their answers.

+ **Make up your own family game:** For example, for Bible Verses, write Scripture verses on index cards such as, "*This is the day the* LORD *has made*" (Psalm 118:24 NKJV), "*The* LORD *bless you and keep you*" (Numbers 6:24), or "*Trust in the* LORD *with all your heart*" (Proverbs 3:5). On one side of the card, write a few words from the verse; on the other side, write the whole verse. Show them the first two or three words of the verse and then have your child finish the rest of the verse. Whenever they finish the verse correctly, they get to put a penny, a dime, or whatever you decide in a jar. They can use the money to purchase something at the local Christian store or give the money to the needy, which will motivate them to play the game and learn more Bible verses. You can also play Bible Words, with a word on the front of the card and the meaning on the back. You can also connect the words to biblical stories.

+ **Presentation folder:** Help your children make a presentation folder labeled "Love for Jesus." Place drawings in their folder or help them write Bible verses. Take pictures of them doing things "for Jesus," like cleaning up their toys, helping their grandparents, or feeding the family pet. Then place the photos in the folder. *"Truly I tell you, whatever you did for one of the least of these brothers and sisters of mine, you did for me"* (Matthew 25:40). At the end of the month, have the family sit down and listen to your children give their presentations. Be very enthusiastic and tell them how happy they made Jesus and how much you loved their presentation. *Enthusiasm* comes from the Greek word *enthousiasmós*, meaning "divine inspiration."

+ **Emotional teaching tools:** Engage your child's emotions to help solidify a biblical concept. To explain the meaning of temptation, place a piece of cake on the table and tell your child not to eat it, or place a bag of candy on the table and tell them they can have the candy or give it to a child in need.[99] Discuss their feelings and options. Afterward, enjoy the sweet treat together.

I am sure you can think of many other ways help connect your children's hearts to Jesus. Be creative and remember to have fun!

READY, SET, ACTION!

Do you know what the stories of Hercules and Jesus have in common? New Testament scholar Joseph R. Dodson notes both claimed to be born of a virgin, escaped death as infants, were commissioned for divine duties, overcame temptation from supernatural forces, were called "son of God/god," were servants, were betrayed by loved ones who hung themselves in remorse, and

---

99. Bruce Barry, et al., *If Disney Ran Your Children's Ministry* (JBD Publishing, 2016), 145.

proclaimed, "It is finished" before they died.[100] Likewise, the story of Superman borrowed from the Gospels too. Superman's father sent him to earth to help save humanity. Superman was raised in an obscure place called Smallville, Kansas, and tried to hide his identity as he used his miraculous powers against evil. Hercules and Superman emulate the one true hero, Jesus Christ.

Does your child like superheroes? In their book *Hollywood Heroes: How Your Favorite Movies Reveal God*,[101] Frank Turek and his son Zach offer philosophical and biblical insights for those who watch superhero movies. Look for ways to incorporate playtime with the best superhero the world has ever known, Jesus. *Bibleman*, an excellent series for children ages five to twelve, is based upon wearing the armor of God (see Ephesians 6:11) and teaching children how the Word of God will help defeat the evil schemes of Satan.[102] Our children are warriors going to boot camp. They need to understand what armor to wear for protection. Be sure to incorporate prayer because *"the devil prowls around like a roaring lion looking for someone to devour"* (1 Peter 5:8).

CHILDREN LEARN THROUGH PLAY AND INTERACTION

Use various tools, props, and materials. Whether they are elaborate or simple, these will help children tangibly learn biblical truths and reinforce biblical concepts through memorization and physical action. If you are able, record their playtime. Children love to see and hear themselves. This makes learning fun and helps with retention as they watch what has been recorded. Here are a few Bible stories you can use to instruct children in fun, creative ways:

---

100. Joseph R. Dodson, "How 'bout Hercules?", *Bible Study Magazine*, May/June 2020, 13.
101. Frank and Zach Turek, *Hollywood Heroes: How Your Favorite Movies Reveal God* (Colorado Springs, CO: NavPress, 2022).
102. bibleman.com.

+ **Noah's Ark (Genesis 7)** — Little ones will enjoy taking their stuffed animals and lining them up to enter the ark. The ark can be a large cardboard box that they decorate to look like a large boat. After the animals are loaded two by two into the ark, take a spray bottle of water and make it rain. Then make a rainbow out of cardboard and markers. Hold the rainbow over the ark as the animals come out two by two.

+ **The Good Samaritan (Luke 10:30–37)** — Bandages, toilet paper, paper towels, and real cloth wraps can be used for this story. Children can also draw a picture or write a get-well card. Act out the scene and use ketchup for the blood on the boo-boo.

+ **The Lost Sheep (Matthew 18:10–14)** — For any story involving sheep, use glue and cotton balls to make the sheep. A dish towel wrapped around the forehead can be a simple costume for a shepherd.

+ **Parable of the Lost Coins (Luke 15:8–10)** — Use an old purse, old shoes, dress-up clothes and hide some coins. Then act out the story and help your child find the coins and put them in her purse for safekeeping. At church, have her put the coins in the collection box.

+ **Parable of the Sower (Matthew 13:1–23)** — Take your children outside. Show them soft soil, hard soil, and rocky soil. Let them see what grows out of good soil such as grass and flowers. Show them poor soil, such as a weed coming up between cracks in the sidewalk. Take bird seed to feed the birds; even if no birds come, your children will still remember the seeds that were a part of the story. Words in action help children retain the lessons being taught.

+ **Jesus Feeds Five Thousand (Mark 6:39–44)** — Take your little one fishing and bring a picnic lunch to share. Explain how Jesus fed 5,000 people with one little boy's lunch of five small loaves of bread and two small fish. You can purchase plastic toys of fish and bread to illustrate the story as you share your picnic lunch.

+ **Healing of the Blind Man at Bethsaida (Mark 8:22–26)** — Have your child place a blindfold over your eyes. He can pretend to spit on your eyes. When he takes off your blindfold, squint your eyes, and tell him that you see trees. Then have him place his hands back on your eyes and say a prayer for healing. When he removes his hands, you can exclaim, "I can see you! Praise Jesus!"

+ **Tower of Babel (Genesis 11:1–9)** — Use toy blocks or sponges to build the tower. Then have your children knock the tower down. Have them speak jibber jabber to simulate foreign languages.

+ **Wall of Jericho (Joshua 6:1–27)** — Use toy blocks or sponges to build the wall of Jericho. You can use a box to prop the wall up for support. Have your children walk around the wall singing "Joshua Fought the Battle of Jericho." Then for the seventh and final time around, have them blow horns as you knock down the walls.

+ **Finding Baby Moses (Exodus 2:1–10)** — Put a baby doll on a float in the pool or in a plastic bowl in the bathtub. As Moses floats down the Nile, tell the story of how he was saved when he was taken out of the water. Then dry the doll off and have your little princess bring him into her castle.

+ **Proverbs 1:8–9** — *"Listen, my son, to your father's instruction and do not forsake your mother's teaching. They are a garland to grace your head and a chain to adorn your neck."* Every time your children obey a directive given by you, take a small rectangular piece of construction paper in various colors and write what they did, such as made their bed, fed the dog, or picked up their toys. Make loops to form a paper chain. Once they have a chain long enough, they can wear it proudly around their neck. Save the chains and pin them onto a corkboard for them to see their accomplishments saved as a piece of art.

INCORPORATING JESUS INTO EVERYDAY LESSONS

You can also use the Bible to help children learn colors, the alphabet, and numbers. For example:

+ Jesus created all earthly things with the Father. He created **green** trees, grass, and various plants.

+ The letter *F* is for forgiveness. Jesus **forgives** us for our sins.

+ There is one God in **three persons**: God the Father, God the Son, and God the Holy Spirit. This may be difficult for children to understand, but again, you are *preparing the soil* for *seeds to be planted* by building a vocabulary and a category in their minds.

Incorporate Jesus-themed days or events to help them learn the days of the week, months of the year, and special holidays.

God's Word can be connected to His creation through museums, observatories, and nature walks. Nature is one of the most outstanding classrooms in the world to learn about God's creativity, purpose, provision, and power.

Another way to connect to the Lord is by reading the biographies of people who have lived well in Christ and made a difference because of their faith in Him and His abounding grace.

God has provided us with many ways and tools to help connect our children's hearts and minds to Christ.

CONCLUSION

Knowing that you have a formal promise or assurance that certain conditions will be met or fulfilled can free you to become the very best spiritual leader for your family. Some people claim there are no guarantees in life, but God's Word is both a promise and a guarantee. If we diligently *prepare a rich soil* and *plant seeds* of righteousness to the best of our ability, we will give our children the best foundation to build their lives for Christ. If we incorporate the techniques, principles, and directives often, we will raise the next generation to bring the kingdom of heaven to earth, becoming the greatest warriors for God.

Christianity is being attacked on every imaginable level. Children are walking away from their faith at an alarming rate. Like Esther, you have been chosen for such a time as this! (See Esther 4:14.) God will declare, *"Well done, good and faithful servant!"* (Matthew 25:23) as He witnesses our children become adults who stand firmly against evil. They will receive the promise of eternal life and abundant blessings. They will build their foundation of faith on the cornerstone of the One who is the creator of all creation.

We have been given great gifts—our children, created in the image of God. It is our responsibility to train them well, to the best of our God-given abilities and talents, day by day and moment by moment, based upon the Word of God.

One of the most important things we can do as parents is to prepare our children to fight against the anti-Christian culture they will inevitably face. We need to instill in them a love for God and His Word and a desire to stand firm in their faith, no matter what happens. We need to instruct them how to think critically about the world around them and stand up for what is right, even when it is unpopular.

We also need to model for them what it looks like to live out our faith boldly and in love with God. We need to be intentional about sharing our faith with others and about living in such a way that others can see Christ in us. If we do these things, then we can be confident that our children will be equipped to fight the good fight and ultimately triumph in their faith.

I pray that you and your children will obtain godly wisdom, great discernment, faith to replace all doubt, and the ability to silence the voice of the enemy. I pray your home will reflect the love of God and will be the training ground to instill truth, love, and faith that lasts a lifetime.

I pray that you will be able to instill in your children a love for God and a desire to follow Him. I encourage you to explore all the resources available to you. I pray that you will find the strength and wisdom to raise your children in faith, and that they will grow to be strong, confident, and faithful adults.

There will be no words to adequately describe the feeling you will have when you sit at the heavenly banquet table and see your children face to face, enjoying all the heavenly blessings while worshipping Jesus for all eternity. Raising kids to follow Christ is all about the salvation of our children and the preservation of our faith.

QUESTIONS FOR REFLECTION

CHAPTER 1 – THE PERFECT CORNERSTONE AND FOUNDATION

1. What steps have you taken so far to help solidify a strong foundation in Christ in your child?

2. List the similarities between the Sand Palace and Matthew 7:24–27.

3. What do Jeremiah, King David, Isaiah, and Timothy all have in common?

4. Why is it important to *prepare the soil?*

5. What childhood memories do you have of Jesus helping you or guiding you?

CHAPTER 2 – IT'S ALWAYS THE RIGHT TIME

1. What do the seeds found in the tombs of the Egyptian pharaohs tell you about God and His provision?

2. How can you prepare the soil for your child three to six months before your baby is born?

3. What can you do to prepare the soil for your child from birth up to age three?

4. What can you do to plant seeds of biblical wisdom in your child from ages four through seven?

CHAPTER 3 – THE DIVINE PARENTING MANUAL

1. What is the *Shema* and why was it important to the Jews in the first century? How does it apply to us today?

2. List some of the commands to teach the next generation, according to Psalm 78:1–8 and Psalm 145:3–7.

3. What are some ways you can demonstrate your love and devotion to God's commands?

4. What are some ways you can help your children remember to praise the Lord?

5. How can one love God with **all** their heart, **all** their soul, and **all** their mind?

CHAPTER 4 – MAKING OBEDIENCE EASIER THROUGH DISCIPLINE

1. What is the difference between guilt and shame? What effect can guilt have on a child? What effect can shame have on a child?

2. What problems arise when one is not consistent in disciplining a child? List some of the ways you can be more consistent in your discipline.

3. Why is transforming a child's heart better than behavior modification?

4. How did King David fail as a parent? What were the outcomes for his children? List the Bible verses.

5. Why do you think it is important to balance discipline with loving guidance?

CHAPTER 5 – CONTINUED CHARACTER DEVELOPMENT FOR OBEDIENT HEART TRANSFORMATION

1. Why should dishonor and disrespect be dealt with swiftly? List ways you have seen your child be disrespectful. List ways in which *you* have been disrespectful to your child.

2. What's the difference between intrinsic and extrinsic motivation? How can you use both to help children learn how to make the right choices?

3. How is positive reinforcement better than threats of punishment?

4. Other than teaching children the importance of earning money or rewards, what other ways can parents handle their children's attitudes of entitlement?

5. Why is it important not to rescue your child from every playmate or bully?

CHAPTER 6 – BUILDING A STRONG CHRISTIAN FOUNDATION

1. What does the word *indoctrination* mean? Why is it not a form of brainwashing?

2. What is the meaning of Christian doctrine? Highlight key words and phrases.

3. What are your child's God-given gifts? What can you do to help them cultivate their gifts to benefit God's kingdom on earth?

4. Why is playtime important for a child? What is sacred play? What can you do to create a sacred play area?

5. What do *ethos*, *pathos*, and *logos* mean? Why are they important to understand when it comes to teaching biblical principles to children?

CHAPTER 7 – PRACTICAL METHODS FOR CONNECTING CHILDREN TO JESUS

1. What is the meaning of Mark 10:15?

2. What does the Greek word *brephos* mean, and to what age does it refer?

3. What correlation do you see regarding your dependence on Jesus and your child's dependence on you?

4. Make a tentative outline for your parenting plan.

5. List some ways you can incorporate Jesus and His Word into your children's lives.

CHAPTER 8 – CULTIVATING TRUST IN GOD AND PARENTAL GUIDANCE

1. What bullet points stood out to you regarding fear and why?

2. How does your child see you handling fearful situations?

3. List the ways you can help your child conquer fear.

4. Why do you think it is more important to tell children to love and forgive others instead of telling them to be happy?

5. List the ways you demonstrate love and care for your child and other children.

CHAPTER 9 – HELPING TO SHAPE A GODLY WORLDVIEW

1. When does a child start to formulate their worldview? How do you think a worldview starts to form at this age?

2. According to this chapter, what are some ways to incorporate Jesus into your everyday routine with your children?

3. What is the difference and the similarity between a faith lesson and a moral lesson?

4. Write a plan for creating spiritual playrooms for your children. How many stations will you have? What Bible stories and toys will you incorporate?

5. How can you incorporate one-on-one time with your children to help formulate their worldview?

CHAPTER 10 – WHY DO WE BELIEVE WHAT WE BELIEVE?

1. What does the word *apologetics* mean?

2. Why is it important for your children to learn how to defend their faith in a loving manner?

3. What are the four questions a worldview must answer? Why must they be answered? What are the three factors

a worldview needs in order to work? Give examples of each.

4. What does this chapter state regarding absolute truth?

5. Write down Bible verses that tell us God's Word is true.

CHAPTER 11 – INSTILLING VIRTUES IN CHILDREN

1. List the virtues described in 2 Peter 1:5–8 in a logical progression. Why do you think this progression is important?

2. Describe the five virtues you believe are the most important and why.

3. In what ways have you taught your children to be virtuous?

4. List three of your favorite psalms regarding the *Rock*. What surprised you about these Scriptures?

5. Describe various ways you can exhibit virtuous character traits in the daily habits of family life.

CHAPTER 12 – INSTILLING FRUIT OF THE SPIRIT

1. How will you explain to your children the difference between love and *agape* love? Why is it important to do so?

2. List the various words that describe joy. Which one do you like best and why?

3. Which fruit of the Spirit do you feel may be lacking in your family? What can you do to try to instill more of that fruit?

4. How do you think the fruit of the Spirit and virtues work together?

5. How can teaching children self-control help them exhibit more fruit of the Spirit?

CHAPTER 13 – HAVE FUN LEARNING TOGETHER

1. What is the greatest combination of tools to build a strong foundation in Christ?

2. What does *intentional parenting* mean?

3. Why is a mission statement important?

4. Write a mission statement for your family. List five implementation suggestions that you found new and promising.

BIBLIOGRAPHY

---, "The Learning Pyramid," *Education Corner: Education That Matters*, www.educationcorner.com/the-learning-pyramid.html.

Achor, Shawn, *The Happiness Advantage: How a Positive Brain Fuels Success in Work and Life* (New York: Crown Currency, 2010).

Alcorn, Randy, *Happiness* (Carol Stream, IL: Tyndale House Publishers, 2015).

Alcorn, Randy, *Heaven* (Chicago, IL: Tyndale House Publishers, 2004).

Barna, George, *Raising Spiritual Champions: Nurturing Your Child's Heart, Mind and Soul* (Glendale, AZ: Arizona Christian University Press & Fedd Books, 2023).

Barna, George, *Revolutionary Parenting: What the Research Shows Really Works* (Carol Stream, IL: Tyndale 2007).

Barna, George, *Transforming Children into Spiritual Champions* (Ventura, CA: Regal Books, 2003).

Barry, Bruce, et al., *If Disney Ran Your Children's Ministry* (JBD Publishing, 2016), 145.

Bengston, Michelle, *Breaking Anxiety's Grip: How to Reclaim the Peace God Promises* (Grand Rapids, MI: Revell, 2019).

Bradley, Reb, *Child Training Tips: What I Wish I Knew When My Children Were Young* (Washington, DC: WND Books, 2014).

Brekus, Catherine A., "Children of Wrath, Children of Grace: Jonathan Edwards and the Puritan Culture of Child Rearing," in *The Child in Christian Thought*, ed. Marcia J. Bunge (Grand Rapids, MI: Wm. B. Eerdmans Publishing Co. 2001).

Carnegie, Dale, *How to Win Friends & Influence People* (New York: Pocket Books, 1998).

Chapman, Gary and Arlene Pellicane, *Growing Up Social: Raising Relational Kids in a Screen-Driven World* (Chicago, IL: Northfield Publishing, 2014).

Christian, Pamela, *Revive Your Life! Rest for Your Anxious Heart* (Yorba Linda, CA: Protocol, Ltd., 2017).

Clarkson, Sally, *Awaking Wonder: Opening Your Child's Heart to the Beauty of Learning* (Bloomington, IN: Bethany House Publishers, 2020).

Cohen, Larry, "Shame: The Oft-Neglected Ingredient in Social Anxiety," December 22, 2022, National Social Anxiety Center, nationalsocialanxietycenter.com/2022/12/22/shame-oft-neglected-ingredient-in-social-anxiety.

Comer, Phil and Diane, *Raising Passionate Jesus Followers: The Power of Intentional Parenting* (Grand Rapids, MI: Zondervan, 2018).

Crain, Natasha, *Talking with Your Kids about God: 30 Conversations Every Christian Parent Must Have* (Grand Rapids, MI: Baker Books, 2017).

Dean, Jennifer Kennedy, *Seek: 28 Days to Extraordinary Prayer* (Birmingham, AL: New Hope Publishers, 2019).

Dodson, Joseph R., "How 'bout Hercules?", *Bible Study Magazine*, May/June 2020.

Eliot, Lise, *What's Going on in There? How the Brain and Mind Develop in the First Five Years of Life* (New York: Bantam Books, 1999).

Geisler, Norman L. and Frank Turek, *I Don't Have Enough Faith to Be an Atheist* (Wheaton, IL: Crossway, 2004).

Gentry, J. Richard, *Raising Confident Readers: How to Teach Your Child to Read and Write—from Baby to Age 7* (Cambridge, MA: Da Capo Press, 2010).

Ham, Ken, *Ready to Return? The Need for a Fundamental Shift in Church Culture to Save a Generation* (Green Forest, AR: New Leaf Publishing Group, 2015).

Harders, Angela, *Gospel-Based Parenting: A Biblical Study on Discipline and Discipling* (Unicorn Publishing Group, 2019).

Hayford, Jack W., *Blessing Your Children: Give the Gift that Will Change Their Lives Forever* (Bloomington, IN: Chosen Books, 2016).

Hellman, Rick, "Study Shows Language Development Starts in the Womb," University of Kansas, July 18, 2017, news.ku.edu/2017/07/13/study-shows-language-development-starts-womb.

Hendricks, Howard, *Teaching to Change Lives: Seven Proven Ways to Make Your Teaching Come Alive* (New York, NY: Multnomah, 1987).

Hubbard, Ginger, *I Can't Believe You Just Said That! Biblical Wisdom for Taming Your Child's Tongue* (Nashville, TN: Nelson Books, 2018).

I Can Only Imagine, directed by Andrew and Jon Erwin (2018; Lionsgate/Roadside Attractions).

Keeley, Robert J., *Helping Our Children Grow in Faith: How the Church Can Nurture the Spiritual Development of Kids* (Grand Rapids, MI: Baker Publishing Group, 2008).

Koch, Kathy, *8 Great Smarts: Discover and Nurture Your Child's Intelligences* (Chicago, IL: Moody Publishers, 2016).

Kock, Kathy, *Start with the Heart: How to Motivate Your Kids to Be Compassionate, Responsible, and Brave (Even When You're Not Around)* (Chicago, IL: Moody Publishers, 2019).

Koukl, Gregory, *Tactics: A Game Plan for Discussing Your Christian Convictions* (Grand Rapids, MI: Zondervan 2009).

Lavender, Julie, *365 Ways to Love Your Child: Turning Little Moments into Lasting Memories* (Grand Rapids, MI: Revell, 2020).

Levenson, Eric, "This home on Mexico Beach survived Hurricane Michael. That's no coincidence," *CNN*, October 16, 2018, www.cnn.com/2018/10/15/us/mexico-beach-house-hurricane-trnd/index.html.

Lotz, Anne Graham, "The Wonderful Someone," *Hugh's News*, February 14, 2019, www.hughsnews.com/newsletter-posts/the-wonderful-someone-by-anne-graham-lotz.

Lutzer, Erwin W., *How to Break a Stubborn Habit* (Eugene, OR: Harvest House Publishers, 2017).

Lynum, Eryn, *Rooted in Wonder: Nurturing Your Family's Faith Through God's Creation* (Grand Rapids, MI: Kregel Publications, 2023).

Manser, Martin H., et al., *Dictionary of Bible Themes: The Accessible and Comprehensive Tool for Topical Studies* (London: Logos Bible Software, 2009).

Markham, Laura, *Peaceful Parent, Happy Kids: How to Stop Yelling and Start Connecting* (New York: Penguin Group, 2012).

May, Scottie, "The Contemplative-Reflective Model," in *Perspectives on Children's Spiritual Formation: 4 Views*, ed. Michael J. Anthony (Nashville, TN: Broadman & Holman Publishers, 2006).

May, Scottie, et al., *Children Matter: Celebrating Their Place in the Church, Family, and Community* (Grand Rapids, MI: Wm. B. Eerdmans Publishing Co., 2005).

Mcleod, Saul, "Kohlberg's Stages of Moral Development," *Simply Psychology*, August 3, 2023, www.simplypsychology.org/kohlberg.html.

Mcleod, Saul, "Vygotsky's Zone of Proximal Development and Scaffolding," *Simply Psychology*, May 14, 2023, www.simplypsychology.org/Zone-of-Proximal-Development.html.

Mercer, Joyce Ann, *Welcoming Children: A Practical Theology of Childhood* (St. Louis, MO: Chalice Press, 2005).

Miller, Lisa, PhD, *The Awakened Brain: The New Science of Spirituality and Our Quest for an Inspired Life* (New York: Penguin Random House, LLC, 2021).

Morgenthaler, Shirley K., *Right from the Start: A Parent's Guide to the Young Child's Faith Development* (St. Louis, MO: Concordia Publishing House, 2001).

Mulvihill, Josh, *Preparing Children for Marriage: How to Teach God's Good Design for Marriage, Sex, Purity, and Dating* (Phillipsburg, NJ: P&R Publishing, 2017).

Packer, J. I., *Concise Theology: A Guide to Historic Christian Beliefs* (Wheaton, IL: Tyndale House, 1993).

Rayner, Victoria, "12 Virtues Introduced by Aristotle – the master of those who know," *Aesthetic Healing Mindset*, June 12, 2011, aesthetichealingmindset.wordpress.com/2011/06/12/4706.

Reid, Vincent M., et al., "The Human Fetus Preferentially Engages with Face-like Visual Stimuli," *Current Biology*, June 8, 2017, doi.org/10.1016/j.cub.2017.05.044.

Saint Chrysostom, "Homilies on Ephesians, XVI," ed. Dr. Philip Schaff, *Saint Chrysostom: Homilies on Galatians, Ephesians, Philippians, Colossians, Thessalonians, Timothy, Titus, and Philemon*, vol. 13 (New York: Charles Scribner's Sons, 1905).

Schneider, Joy A., *How to Keep Grief from Stealing Your Destiny* (Fort Collins, CO: Water of Life Unlimited 2016).

Schuller, Bobby, *Change Your Thoughts, Change Your World: How Life-Giving Thoughts Can Unlock Your Destiny* (Nashville, TN: Nelson Books, 2019).

Sleeth, Matthew, *Reforesting Faith: What Trees Teach Us About the Nature of God and His Love for Us* (New York: WaterBrook, 2019).

Spence, Gerry, *How to Argue and Win Every Time* (New York: St. Martin's Press, 1995).

Stonehouse, Catherine and Scottie May, *Listening to Children on the Spiritual Journey: Guidance for Those Who Teach and Nurture* (Grand Rapids, MI: Baker Publishing Group, 2010).

Strohl, Jane E., "The Child in Luther's Theology: 'For What Purpose Do We Older Folks Exist, Other Than to Care for...the Young?'" in *The Child in Christian Thought*, ed. Marcia J. Bunge (Grand Rapids, MI: Wm. B. Eerdmans Publishing Co., 2001).

Turansky, Scott and Joanne Miller, *Parenting Is Heart Work* (Colorado Springs, CO: David C. Cook, 2005).

Turansky, Scott and Joanne Miller, *Parenting Is Heart Work: Training Manual* (Lawrenceville, NJ: National Center for Biblical Training, 2015).

Turek, Frank and Zach, *Hollywood Heroes: How Your Favorite Movies Reveal God* (Colorado Springs, CO: NavPress, 2022).

Van Alstyne, David, "Church Kids Say the Darndest Things," David Van Alstyne blog, https://www.davidvanalstyne.com/pg-kidschurchsay.html.

Wermke, Kathleen, quoted by Robert Emmerich, "Language begins with the very first cry," *Informationsdienst Wissenschaft* (The Science Information Service), May 11, 2009, idw-online.de/de/news342774.

White, David A. R., *Between Heaven and Hollywood: Chasing Your God-Given Dream* (Grand Rapids, MI: Zondervan, 2016).

White, Kevin, *Audacious Generosity: How to Experience, Receive, and Give More Than You Ever Thought Possible* (Carol Stream, IL: Tyndale House Publishers, 2020).

Yates, Susan Alexander, *Cousin Camp: A Grandparent's Guide to Creating Fun, Faith, and Memories That Last* (Grand Rapids, MI: Revell, 2020).

ADDITIONAL RESOURCES:

answersingenesis.org
bibleman.com
hslda.org
raisingchristiankids.com
schoolhouserocked.com
www.summit.org/about
www.thehomeschoolawakening.com

BIBLE INDEX

Symbols

ABOUT THE AUTHOR

Lee Ann Mancini is passionate about helping children build a lifelong, unshakeable foundation in Jesus. She is the founder and CEO of Raising Christian Kids Inc., a nonprofit dedicated to equipping parents and caregivers with the tools they need to become the best spiritual leaders for their children.

Lee Ann is a wife and the mother of two grown children. Her award-winning children's books and animated series, *Sea Kids*, are based on the stories she wrote for her young children about cute sea creatures who learn about God's morals and values through everyday childhood experiences.

Lee Ann's award-winning podcast, *Raising Christian Kids*, is filled with expert parenting advice and wisdom, as well as interviews with nationally and internationally acclaimed Christian experts on parenting and growing up in today's world.

An adjunct professor at South Florida Bible College, she earned two master's degrees from Knox Theological Seminary—in Christian, classical, biblical, and theological studies—and a master's in Christian studies from Trinity Evangelical Divinity School.

Lee Ann has devoted her life to the salvation of children and the preservation of Christianity.